Selected Works of Frits Albers
Volume 4

I0088752

Bound to the Virgin
The Victimhood of Our Blessed Lady
The Glories of the New Eve

Edited by

Frank Calneggia

En Route Books and Media, LLC
Saint Louis, MO

⊕*ENROUTE*
Make the time

En Route Books and Media, LLC
5705 Rhodes Avenue
St. Louis, MO 63109

Contact us at
contactus@enroutebooksandmedia.com

Cover Credit: Sebastian Mahfood from a photo of Michelangelo's *Pietà* (completed in 1499), the famous Renaissance marble sculpture housed in St. Peter's Basilica, Vatican City

ISBN-13: 979-8-88870-438-7
Library of Congress Control Number: 2025947106

Dedication

Dedicated with due humility and filial submission to His Holiness Pope John Paul II in gratitude for writing that magnificent Marian Encyclical *Redemptoris Mater* for the opening of the 1987 Marian Year as the Catholic response to the Humanist call for 'A New World Order' and the Modernist call for 'A New Church'.

October, 1990

Table of Contents

Book II: The Victimhood of Our Blessed Lady...........................113

Book III: The Glories of the New Eve 141

Quotations

#56 Thus Mary, a daughter of Adam, consenting to the divine Word, became the mother of Jesus, the one and only Mediator. Embracing God's salvific will with a full heart and impeded by no sin, she devoted herself totally as a handmaid of the Lord to the person and work of her Son, under Him and with Him, by the grace of almighty God, serving the mystery of redemption. Rightly therefore the holy Fathers see her as used by God not merely in a passive way, but as freely cooperating in the work of human salvation through faith and obedience. For, as St. Irenaeus says, she "being obedient, became the cause of salvation for herself and for the whole human race." Hence not a few of the early Fathers gladly assert in their preaching, "The knot of Eve's disobedience was untied by Mary's obedience; what the virgin Eve bound through her unbelief, the Virgin Mary loosened by her faith." Comparing Mary with Eve, they call her "the Mother of the living," and still more often they say: "death through Eve, life through Mary."

#57 This union of the Mother with the Son in the work of salvation is made manifest from the time of Christ's virginal conception up to His death.

#62 This maternity of Mary in the order of grace began with the consent which she gave in faith at the Annunciation and which she sustained without wavering beneath the cross, and lasts until the eternal fulfillment of all the elect. Taken up to heaven she did not lay aside this salvific duty, but by her constant intercession continued to bring us the gifts of eternal salvation.

#63 By reason of the gift and role of divine maternity, by which she is united with her Son, the Redeemer, and with His singular graces and functions, the Blessed Virgin is also intimately united with the Church. As St. Ambrose taught, the Mother of God is a type of the Church in the order of faith, charity and perfect union with Christ. For in the mystery of the Church, which is itself rightly called mother and virgin, the Blessed Virgin stands out in eminent and singular fashion as exemplar both of virgin and mother.

#65 But while in the most holy Virgin the Church has already reached that perfection whereby she is without spot or wrinkle, the followers of Christ still strive to increase in holiness by conquering sin. And so they turn their eyes to Mary who shines forth to the whole community of the elect as the model of virtues. Piously meditating on her and contemplating her in the light of the Word made man, the Church with reverence enters more intimately into the great mystery of the Incarnation and becomes more and more like her Spouse.

Dogmatic Constitution on the Church
Lumen Gentium
Solemnly Promulgated by His Holiness
Pope Paul VI on November 21, 1964

#11. As we examine the texts of the revised Missal we see how the great Marian themes of the Roman prayerbook have been accepted in perfect doctrinal continuity with the past. Thus, for example, we have the themes of Mary's Immaculate Conception and fullness of grace, the divine motherhood, the unblemished and fruitful virginity, the Temple of the Holy Spirit, Mary's cooperation in the work of her Son, her exemplary sanctity, merciful intercession, Assumption into heaven, maternal Queenship and many other themes. We also see how other themes, in a certain sense new ones, have been introduced in equally perfect harmony with the theological developments of the present day. Thus, for example, we have the theme of Mary and the Church, which has been inserted into the texts of the Missal in a variety of aspects, a variety that matches the many and varied relations that exist between the Mother of Christ and the Church. For example, in the celebration of the Immaculate Conception which texts recognize the beginning of the Church, the spotless Bride of Christ. In the Assumption they recognize the beginning that has already been made and the image of what, for the whole Church, must still come to pass. In the mystery of Mary's motherhood they confess that she is the Mother of the Head and of the members - the holy Mother of God and therefore the provident Mother of the Church.

When the liturgy turns its gaze either to the primitive Church or to the Church of our own days it always finds Mary. In the primitive Church she is seen praying with the apostles; in our own day she is actively present, and the Church desires to live the mystery of Christ with her: "Grant that your Church which with Mary shared Christ's passion may be worthy to share also in his resurrection." She is also seen represented as a voice of praise in unison with which the Church wishes to give glory to God: "...with her [Mary] may we always praise you." And since the liturgy is worship that requires a way of living consistent with it, it asks that devotion to the Blessed Virgin should become a concrete and deeply-felt love for the Church, as is wonderfully expressed in the prayer after Communion in the Mass of September: "...that as we recall the sufferings shared by the Blessed Virgin Mary, we may with the Church fulfill in ourselves what is lacking in the sufferings of Christ."

#20 This union of the Mother and the Son in the work of redemption reaches its climax on Calvary, where Christ "offered himself as the perfect sacrifice to God" (Heb. 9:14) and where Mary stood by the cross (cf. Jn 19:25), "suffering grievously with her only-begotten Son. There she united herself with a maternal heart to His sacrifice, and lovingly consented to the immolation of this victim which she herself had brought forth" and also was "offering to the eternal Father."

Apostolic Exhortation of His Holiness Pope Paul VI
Marialis Cultus
For the Right Ordering and Development of
Devotion to the Blessed Virgin Mary
February 2, 1974

#2. Strengthened by the presence of Christ (cf. Mt. 28:20), the Church journeys through time towards the consummation of the ages and goes to meet the Lord who comes. But on this journey - and I wish to make this point straightaway - she proceeds along the path already trodden by the Virgin Mary, who "advanced in her pilgrimage of faith, and loyally persevered in her union with her Son unto the cross".

#5. The Second Vatican Council, by presenting Mary in the mystery of Christ, also finds the path to a deeper understanding of the mystery of the Church. Mary, as the Mother of Christ, is in a particular way united with the Church, "which the Lord established as his own body." It is significant that the conciliar text places this truth about the Church as the Body of Christ (according to the teaching of the Pauline Letters) in close proximity to the truth that the Son of God "through the power of the Holy Spirit was born of the Virgin Mary." The reality of the Incarnation finds a sort of extension in the mystery of the Church - the Body of Christ. And one cannot think of the reality of the Incarnation without referring to Mary, the Mother of the Incarnate Word.

In these reflections, however, I wish to consider primarily that "pilgrimage of faith" in which "the Blessed Virgin advanced," faithfully preserving her union with Christ. In this way the "twofold bond" which unites the Mother of God with Christ and with the Church takes on historical significance. Nor is it just a question of the Virgin Mother's life-story, of her personal journey of faith and "the better part" which is hers in the mystery of salvation; it is also a question of the history of the whole People of God, of all those who take part in the same "pilgrimage of faith."

The Council expresses this when it states in another passage that Mary "has gone before", "becoming a model of the Church in the matter of faith, charity and perfect union with Christ". This "going before" as a figure or model is in reference to the intimate mystery of the Church, as she actuates and accomplishes her own saving mission by uniting in herself - as Mary did - the qualities of mother and virgin. She is a virgin who "keeps whole and pure the fidelity she has pledged to her Spouse" and "becomes herself a mother," for "she brings forth to a new and immortal life children who are conceived of the Holy Spirit and born of God."

#6. The pilgrimage of faith indicates the interior history, that is, the story of souls. But it is also the story of all human beings, subject here on earth to transitoriness, and part of the historical dimension. In the following reflections we wish to concentrate first of all on the present, which in itself is not yet history, but which nevertheless is constantly forming it, also in the sense of the history of salvation. Here there opens up a broad prospect, within which the Blessed Virgin Mary continues to "go before" the People of God. Her exceptional pilgrimage of faith represents a constant point of reference for the Church, for individuals and for communities, for peoples and nations and, in a sense, for all humanity. It is indeed difficult to encompass and measure its range.

The Council emphasizes that the Mother of God is already the eschatological fulfillment of the Church: "In the most holy Virgin the Church has already reached that perfection whereby she exists without spot or wrinkle (cf. Eph. 5:27)"; and at the same time the Council says that "the followers of Christ still strive to increase in holiness by conquering sin, and so they raise their eyes to Mary, who shines forth to the whole community of the elect as a model of the virtues." The pilgrimage of faith no longer belongs to the Mother of the Son of God: glorified at the side of her Son in heaven, Mary has already crossed the threshold between faith and that vision which is "face to face" (1 Cor. 13:12). At the same time, however, in this eschatological fulfillment, Mary does not cease to be the "Star of the Sea" (Maris Stella) for all those who are still on the journey of faith. If they lift their eyes to her from their earthly existence, they do so because "the Son whom she brought forth is he whom God placed as the first-born among many brethren (Rom. 8:29)," and also because "in the birth and development" of these brothers and sisters "she cooperates with a maternal love."

#8. Mary is definitively introduced into the mystery of Christ through this event: the Annunciation by the angel. This takes place at Nazareth, within the concrete circumstances of the history of Israel, the people which first received God's promises. The divine messenger says to the Virgin: "Hail, full of grace, the Lord is with you" (Lk. 1:28). Mary "was greatly troubled at the saying, and considered in her mind what sort of greeting this might be" (Lk. 1:29): what could those extraordinary words mean, and in particular the expression "full of grace" (kecharitoméne).

If we wish to meditate together with Mary on these words, and especially on the expression "full of grace," we can find a significant echo in the very passage from the Letter to the Ephesians quoted above. And if after the announcement of the heavenly messenger the Virgin of Nazareth is also called "blessed among women" (cf. Lk. 1:42), it is because of that blessing with which "God the Father" has filled us "in the heavenly places, in Christ." It is a spiritual blessing which is meant for all people and which bears in itself fullness and universality ("every blessing"). It flows from that love which, in the Holy Spirit, unites the consubstantial Son to the Father. At the same time, it is a blessing poured out through Jesus Christ upon human history until the end: upon all people. This blessing, however, refers to Mary in a special and exceptional degree: for she was greeted by Elizabeth as "blessed among women."

The double greeting is due to the fact that in the soul of this "daughter of Sion" there is manifested, in a sense, all the "glory of grace," that grace which "the Father...has given us in his beloved Son." For the messenger greets Mary as "full of grace"; he calls her thus as if it were her real name. He does not call her by her proper earthly name: Miryam (= Mary), but by this new name: "full of grace." What does this name mean? Why does the archangel address the Virgin of Nazareth in this way?

In the language of the Bible "grace" means a special gift, which according to the New Testament has its source precisely in the Trinitarian life of God himself, God who is love (cf. 1 Jn. 4:8). The fruit of this love is "the election" of which the Letter to the Ephesians speaks. On the part of God, this election is the eternal desire to save man through a sharing in his own life (cf. 2 Pt. 1:4) in Christ: it is salvation through a sharing in supernatural life. The effect of this eternal gift, of this grace of man's election by God, is like a seed of holiness, or a spring which rises in the soul as a gift from God himself, who through grace gives life and holiness to those who are chosen. In this way there is fulfilled, that is to say there comes about, that "blessing" of man "with every spiritual blessing," that "being his adopted sons and daughters...in Christ," in him who is eternally the "beloved Son" of the Father.

When we read that the messenger addresses Mary as "full of grace," the Gospel context, which mingles revelations and ancient promises, enables us to understand that among all the "spiritual blessings in Christ" this is a special "blessing." In the mystery of Christ she is present even "before the creation of the world," as the one whom the Father "has chosen" as Mother of his Son in the Incarnation. And, what is more, together with the Father, the Son has chosen her, entrusting her eternally to the Spirit of holiness. In an entirely special and exceptional way Mary is united to Christ, and similarly she is eternally loved in this "beloved Son," this Son who is of one being with the Father, in whom is concentrated all the "glory of grace." At the same time, she is and remains perfectly open to this "gift from above" (cf. Jas. 1:17). As the Council teaches, Mary "stands out among the poor and humble of the Lord, who confidently await and receive salvation from him."

#9. If the greeting and the name "full of grace" say all this, in the context of the angel's announcement they refer first of all to the election of Mary as Mother of the Son of God. But at the same time the "fullness of grace" indicates all the supernatural munificence from which Mary benefits by being chosen and destined to be the Mother of Christ. If this election is fundamental for the accomplishment of God's salvific designs for humanity, and if the eternal choice in Christ and the vocation to the dignity of adopted children is the destiny of everyone, then the election of Mary is wholly exceptional and unique. Hence also the singularity and uniqueness of her place in the mystery of Christ.

The divine messenger says to her: "Do not be afraid, Mary, for you have found favor with God. And behold, you will conceive in your womb and bear a son, and you shall call his name Jesus. He will be great, and will be called the Son of the Most High" (Lk. 1:30-32). And when the Virgin, disturbed by that extraordinary greeting, asks: "How shall this be, since I have no husband?" she receives from the angel the confirmation and explanation of the preceding words. Gabriel says to her: "The Holy Spirit will come upon you, and the power of the Most High will overshadow you; therefore the child to be born will be called holy, the Son of God" (Lk. 1:35).

The Annunciation, therefore, is the revelation of the mystery of the Incarnation at the very beginning of its fulfillment on earth. God's salvific giving of himself and his life, in some way to all creation but directly to man, reaches one of its high points in the mystery of the Incarnation. This is indeed a high point among all the gifts of grace conferred in the history of man and of the universe: Mary is "full of grace," because it is precisely in her that the Incarnation of the Word, the hypostatic union of the Son of God with human nature, is accomplished and fulfilled. As the Council says, Mary is "the Mother of the Son of God. As a result she is also the favorite daughter of the Father and the temple of the Holy Spirit. Because of this gift of sublime grace, she far surpasses all other creatures, both in heaven and on earth."

#11. In the salvific design of the Most Holy Trinity, the mystery of the Incarnation constitutes the superabundant fulfillment of the promise made by God to man after original sin, after that first sin whose effects oppress the whole earthly history of man (cf. Gen. 3:15). And so, there comes into the world a Son, "the seed of the woman" who will crush the evil of sin in its very origins: "he will crush the head of the serpent." As we see from the words of the Protogospel, the victory of the woman's Son will not take place without a hard struggle, a struggle that is to extend through the whole of human history. The "enmity," foretold at the beginning, is confirmed in the Apocalypse (the book of the final events of the

Church and the world), in which there recurs the sign of the "woman," this time "clothed with the sun" (Rev. 12:1).

Mary, Mother of the Incarnate Word, is placed at the very center of that enmity, that struggle which accompanies the history of humanity on earth and the history of salvation itself. In this central place, she who belongs to the "weak and poor of the Lord" bears in herself, like no other member of the human race, that "glory of grace" which the Father "has bestowed on us in his beloved Son," and this grace determines the extraordinary greatness and beauty of her whole being. Mary thus remains before God, and also before the whole of humanity, as the unchangeable and inviolable sign of God's election, spoken of in Paul's letter: "in Christ...he chose us...before the foundation of the world,...he destined us...to be his sons" (Eph. 1:4, 5). This election is more powerful than any experience of evil and sin, than all that "enmity" which marks the history of man. In this history Mary remains a sign of sure hope.

> Encyclical Letter of His Holiness Pope John Paul II
> ***Redemptoris Mater***
> On the Blessed Virgin Mary
> in the life of the Pilgrim Church
> March 25, 1987

#6. Consequently the Immaculate Virgin, who marks *"the very beginning of the Church, Bride of Christ, without spot or wrinkle, shining with beauty"* (Preface), always *precedes* the People of God *in the pilgrimage of faith,* bound for the Kingdom of Heaven (cf. *Lumen Gentium,* n. 58; *Redemptoris Mater,* n. 2).

In Mary's Immaculate Conception the Church sees projected and anticipated in her most noble member, the saving grace of Easter.

In the event of the Incarnation the Church encounters Christ and Mary indissolubly united: "he who is the Church's Lord and Head and she who, uttering the first *fiat* of the New Covenant, prefigures the Church's condition as spouse and mother" (*Redemptoris Mater*, n. 1).

Holy Mass on the Occasion of the 150th Anniversary of
The Dogma of the Immaculate Conception
of the Blessed Virgin Mary.
Homily of John Paul II. 8 December 2004

Preface

This is the fourth volume to be published of *The Selected Works of Frits Albers*, and the first volume in the series to be devoted to his works on Our Lady. Selected for publication in this present volume are the following three books.

Bound to the Virgin
The Victimhood of Our Blessed Lady
The Glories of the New Eve

It is a privelege and a joy to make these books available to a new and wider readership. The exigency for this new publication has become more obvious and pressing after the lapse of years since the original publication of these titles.

The first, *Bound to the Virgin*, documents a global and deceptive religious movement that originated in the late nineteenth century and has its origins in syncretism. With substantial and compelling evidence the author exposes the religious nature of this movement and the subsequent transformation of its objectives into communist political ideals and practices. He is concerned to warn Catholics not to be deceived by either of the two faces of this global entity whose main aim is to destroy Catholic Faith and to subject the entire world to religious, political and economic slavery.

Having dealt with deception the author turns his attention to the Church's teaching on Catholic Faith; Thomism; and Our Lady. Here he is concerned to bring out the nature of Catholic Faith, the bond between Catholic Faith and its seat in the human intellect and how this bond is rightly established and strenghtened by the Philosphy of St. Thomas Aquinas to that unique entity: to what Pope St. Pius X called 'the discipline of the mind'; the interplay between the Supernatural Light of Catholic Faith and clear thinking on the human level.

The author turns to Our Lady, our Mother and our Model for ordering our lives by the Supernatural and natural lights of the discipline of the mind; for Mary, the New Eve of the Redemption, was not deceived by believing the message that came to Her from God. To encourage Catholics to model themselves on Our Lady and to bind themselves to their Mother in Faith, Hope and Love, the author presents the True Devotion of St. Louis de Montfort from the natural and Supernatural perspectives of the discipline of the mind.

From this high point and the blessings and understanding it brings for personal sanctification and salvation, and for avoiding deception, the author offers encouragement, hope and practical means to firstly avoid and then to obtain victory over the evils of the politico-religious deception exposed and analysed in the first part of the book.

The Victimhood of Our Blessed Lady is the shortest of the three books in this present volume. It is composed of four parts: The New Eve; Doctrinal Foundations of the New Eve in Church Documents; The Prayer Life of the Blessed Virgin; The Annunciation and The Incarnation.

This book is a profound exposition of the Mariology of the the Second Vatican Council; which, as the author shows, has its foundation in the Dogmas of the Immaculate Conception and Incarnation, and its culmination in the Dogma of the Assumption. From the homilies one hears on the Feast of the Assumption, even homilies from good orthodox priests, it seems there is little or no comprehension of the means by which Pope Pius XII traced this Dogma to the sources of Revelation, to the Bible. They put before their flocks fitting and most noble reasons (such as the Divine Maternity) for the Assumption of Our Lady into heaven, but which reasons are *not* the actual reason upon which Pope Pius XII based the dogmatic definition.

In order for Catholics to rightly understand the nature of our supernatural existence in the Mystical Body of Christ, it is essential that we understand the Victimhood of Our Blessed Lady and its consequences for us. The author shows that the Victimhood of Our Blessed Lady has its origin in Her Immaculate Conception; its acceptance on Her own behalf and on our behalf at the Annunciation; its consummation at the foot of Cross, and its ultimate perfection in Her Assumption into heaven.

It is the union of Our Blessed Lady with Her Divine Son, the union of the new Eve with the new Adam, in and by which the struggle common to both the Head, the new Adam, and the Mystical Body in the person of Our Lady, the new Eve, to overcome the infernal foe was victorious. The author shows that this common struggle of both the Head, and the Mystical Body in the person of Our Lady subordinated to the Head, is the foundation in Revelation upon which Pope Pius XII based the Assumption of Our Blessed Lady and declared it to be a Dogma, to be believed with Divine and infused Catholic Faith.

With the understanding of the reason for the Assumption of Our Lady, the struggle common to the New Adam and the New Eve firmly established, the consequences for Catholics as the other "seed of the Woman", the other members of the Mystical Body of which Our Lady is both Mother and Model, are brought out with clarity and will give much needed hope and consolation in the troubled and trying circumstances of modern living.

The third book in the present volume has ten sections (I-X) of which the first nine (I-IX) give selected quotes from the Wisdom Literature of the Old Testament. These nine sections, which at various places in the text the author refers to as 'Days' were composed originally as a little novena booklet with the title "The Call For Mary – Echoes of Ancient Centuries." The author subsequently took the Old Testament readings from each day in his novena to Our Lady and reproduced them in their present form in *The Glories of the New Eve.*

There is an ancient rule in the Church about the bible: "the New Testament lies hidden in the Old and the Old is revealed in the New". The author takes this guiding principle to look back into the Wisdom Literature of the Old Testament to make clear for the instruction and consolation of his readers the presence of the future Immaculately Conceived Mother of God in those profound sacred texts centred on a unique Woman who is presented under the aspect of created wisdom.

For each 'Day' the author intersperses meditations and their logical conclusions within and around the sacred texts. If he or she so wishes, the reader could prayerfully read this book on a day by day plan over nine days; for there is much to absorb and upon which to meditate each day. Not only is there a plenitude of beautiful instruction about the person of Our Lady and the only Church conceived in the image and likeness of the New Eve of the Redemption; there is also much to absorb and to think about when the author teaches by contrast: when he contrasts the virginal Marian Catholic Church, and her children of wisdom; with the unwise and undisciplined who populate the festering 'one world church' of darkness forseen and foretold by Pope St. Pius X.

The three books just summarized were first published in the 1980s and 1990s. It is our hope that the present publication of these unique books which were very much a labour of love for their late author, will help and encourage Catholics to know and love their Catholic Faith and what that Faith is; to know and love Our Lady and Our Holy Mother the Catholic Church in order to better know and love our most Holy Redeemer; to learn and understand the basic principles of the Philosophy of St. Thomas Aquinas and the discipline of the mind so as to grasp truth firmly on the human level and to avoid the inevitable deception that comes with crooked thinking; and ultimately to help others, especially their children, to do the same.

Book I

Bound to the Virgin

Frits Albers, Ph.B.

Originally Published
October 1982

On the Feast of the Holy Rosary

Editor's Foreword

When the contents of this book appeared for the first time, it was in the form of printed sheets, as a follow-up (by special request) to a series of ten lectures, delivered by their author, Mr. Frits Albers, to Sydney audiences in 1980. These lectures have since appeared in book form under the title *The Foundations of Our Catholic Faith.*

Initially, then, this present volume was written for people who were familiar with the author's previous work. Desirous to see the invincible bond between the natural light of clear thinking and the supernatural Light of Faith lived out to perfection in one special person: Our Blessed Lady, they felt at the same time the need for a *way of life* in which this perfection could be imitated and made their own. Thus it became inevitable that the whole idea crystallised around the conviction that such an additional lecture would throw an unexpected, powerful light on a particular 'way of life': *the True Devotion of St. Louis Grignion de Montfort.* This explains the original title carried by those earlier sheets: *The True Devotion and the Discipline of the Mind.*

However, there are many Christians who possess a natural curiosity towards anything that is connected to devotion to Our Blessed Lady, and who would like to read a little treatise on Her without being forced to first absorb a ten-lecture series, however beneficial that may be. In preparing his valuable manuscript for print, to cater for this broadening of his readership, the author was forced to develop much more fully in some places what he could

3

naturally expect to be understood in a few words by his erstwhile listeners in Sydney. It will be obvious to people, familiar with the works of Frits Albers, that, in the printed edition of this book, written for people without any acquaintance with the author's previous work, a certain amount of repetition thus became unavoidable. But even where this was necessary, the author has achieved to place before his many devoted readers in a new, fresh and original way what he had already treated more extensively elsewhere, so that even for those familiar with his earlier work, the impact would be invigorating.

In preparing this initial lecture for print, which, as already explained, involved some modification of the original text, it was also decided to change the earlier title to the one carried by this book.

Author's Preface

Convinced that the mind which requested that this treatise on Our Blessed Lady should see the light of day is an *apostolic* mind, prepared to put up with some revision and repetition, necessary for the organic unity of a whole that is to be created out of all this immensely rich material, I have accepted the challenge to prepare this work for print. Conscious of my own limitations I have nevertheless let myself be guided by the over-riding demands made by the Holy See, to take this matter of *the Discipline of the Mind* very seriously indeed, since the absence of it was identified by one Holy Father – Pope St. Pius X – as a sure sign by which the approaching one-world 'church of darkness' can be recognised. (*Our Apostolic Mandate*, 1910.) Does not St. John state in his *Book of Revelation* that "… *the whole world will run after the beast* …" (ch.13, v.3), and does this not reveal for sure, that at one stage the whole world will be in the grip of the most crooked thinking possible?

Since this 'church of darkness', this 'church' of the Second Beast "that looks like the Lamb but speaks like the Dragon" (Rev. ch.13, v.11), is the exact antithesis of the Church of which Our Blessed Lady is the Model and the Proto-type, it must follow by necessity that the Faith of Our Blessed Lady, that Faith which is the antithesis of the 'faith' by which the Beast will be hailed, must have a lot to do with clear thinking; and that both the natural and Supernatural Light were used by Her for the proper ordering of Her life, and all Her actions. It is this organic unity between those two lights, the most formidable thing on this earth, to which Pope St.

Pius X referred as 'the Discipline of the Mind', the absence of which he clearly foresaw and foretold as the hallmark of 'the great apostasy, operating in every country (of his days) towards the establishment of the one-world church of darkness'. (Ibid.)

If this means anything, it means that deception will be rife both during the time of the Beast and in the time of its preparation. But deception is impossible in the Supernatural Light of Catholic Faith, strengthened by clear thinking to that unique entity: *the Discipline of the Mind*. It is therefore necessary to start this treatise with a chapter on a somewhat comprehensive analysis of the massive deception which is part and parcel of the so-called 'religious' world of our times. Hence its inclusion both in the original lecture as in this book.

Deception can be overcome. Since there are many false shepherds and lost sheep in the Catholic fold today, many deceivers and deceived alike, it is instructive to analyse how some withstood deception and overcame it where others floundered. This will be done in the remainder of the book.

The whole story cannot be told in one volume. For additional information, readers are referred to the excellent tapes by Mr. J.W.G. (Wallace) Johnson, of Brisbane, Australia; to a fascinating book by John Cotter: *A Study in Syncretism*, Canadian Intelligence Publications, Canada, 1979; and to my own two books on the subject: *The Foundations of Our Catholic Faith*, and *The Marian Dimension in the Apocalypse of St. John*.

(Ed. *The Foundations of Our Catholic Faith* is published in the *Selected Works of Frits Albers, Volume 3*. En Route Books and Media, 2024.)

Introduction

"Then I saw a second beast; it emerged from the earth. It had two horns like the Lamb, but spoke like the Dragon. This second beast was servant to the first beast, and extended its authority everywhere, making the world and its people worship the first beast ...." (Rev. 13:11-12.)

"And the whole world marvelled and followed the beast. They prostrated themselves before the Dragon because he had given the beast his authority. And they prostrated themselves in front of the beast saying, 'Who can compare with the beast? How could anybody defeat him?'" (Rev.13:3-5.)

"Now a great sign appeared in Heaven: a Woman adorned with the sun, standing on the moon and with the twelve stars on Her head for crown." (Rev.12:1.)

My book is about staying with this Woman, conquering these two beasts.

Chapter One

Deception

OUR LORD has foretold us that, towards the end of time, there would prevail a state of affairs so far removed from His Gospel, that, "if it were possible, even the Elect would be deceived". (Mt.24:24.)

OUR LADY has come down from Heaven to tell us at FATIMA to be on our guard against deception, when She warned us of a world-wide spread of error.

POPE ST. PIUS X has officially taught us, as the Vicar of Christ on earth, that the great movement of apostasy, which he saw operating in every country of his days, would eventually bring about a 'church of darkness', which according to the clear description he gave of this monstrosity, would be a 'church of fraud and deception, as it would use pretexts: the pretexts of freedom and human dignity, to do evil'. (1910.)

POPE PAUL VI has startled us all with his revelation 'that the smoke of Satan was actually finding its way into the Church of God, seeping in through the cracks'.

Even if we assume Our Blessed Saviour could have been referring to another time, the other three people speaking on His behalf and with His authority, have not left us in any doubt as to the times they are referring to, nor of the reality they see in that time; having in mind the Salvation of Souls, and the role Truth plays in that. It would be prudent, then, to take the words of Our Lord to heart as spoken to us, as it is utterly inconceivable that He would have a different view of the present-day realities on our earth, at variance with the one unanimously expressed by the other three witnesses mentioned above, who are not only competent to tell us 'what is in the mind of Christ'; but were also appointed and sent by Our Saviour to speak in His Name, with His Authority.

There are certainly not lacking in our days organisations, movements and streams, all clamouring for the right of our attention, as they are vying with one another in offering us a way out of the turmoil and confusion.

- There is the whole 'encounter movement'.
- There are the never-ending streams of spurious 'apparitions', thriving on the gullibility and disobedience of their numerous followers and promoters.
- There is the false ecumenism with its open 'gospel' that the Catholic Church is defective and in need of a drastic overhaul.
- And for those who like to get away from it all, there is the whole emotional escape of the so-called 'charismatic renewal' with its instant hot-line to the 'spirit' in the make-believe holiness of the neo-gnosticism.

These are but a few examples of the many attempts made by their various adherents in fulfilling Christ's prophecy: "Take care that no one deceives you; because many will come, using My Name, saying, 'I am the Christ', and they will deceive many". (Mt.24:4-5.) If many of the solutions offered by these agencies are just as defective as the evils they claim to remedy, and if the deceptions associated with them are as world-wide and severe as Our Blessed Lady and Pope St. Pius X have intimated to us, then the reality of this deception 'is in the mind of Christ'. This means not only, that His Catholic Church, His Bride, has been fully alerted by Him to the existence of this evil, but also that, as in previous generations, the Catholic Church has known the solution for more than 100 years in advance, and has revealed it to Her children in plenty of time.

I

The Reality of Deception

Anyone seriously interested in the 600-year systematic breakdown of Thomism with the consequent dismissal of trained clear thinking, need only to study the emergence of the 'One-World Church', and all that led up to its appearance over the last 150 years. The amount of evidence available is staggering; the value for Truth, Salvation of Souls and the Supernatural Life: nil. This history is stacked with *world congresses*, *associations*, *formations of brotherhoods*, *new religions*, *lectures*, *seminars*, *unions*, *world fellowships*, *councils*, *world summits*, etc. etc. They all, without fail or exception, have three things in common, amongst a host of various other undesirable attributes:

(i)   There is not only a deliberate ignoring of the Truth, but also, and even more so, *a studious suppression of the Truth,* which proves that the Truth is known but not wanted: the classic definition of deception.

(ii) They all follow, and even push, at least some major aspect of the Communist line, showing their Marxist origin and worldly aspirations.

(iii) Whatever they may tolerate from Christianity to give themselves some air of respectability, they nevertheless are all intolerant of Catholicism. This has a tremendous bearing on the driving force and global vision behind the one objective: the creation of a one-world 'church'. If true Catholicism has been steadfastly rejected by the Movement over the last 150 years, but a certain brand of 'catholicism' is now being made welcome, then here we have a decisive yardstick by which we can measure how far modernism and teilhardism have broken away from Catholic Unity and Truth to become 'fashionable' and acceptable to the opposition.

If all this is true for the various movements themselves, and can be assumed true for the leaders, it must not be implied that this is clearly understood, or even intended, by the millions of individuals that make up these agglomerates. That they can be sincere, we must admit. That they are misguided and deceived, we must hasten to add. After all, did not the great Pope St. Pius X brand the whole push towards the creation of a 'one-world church' as "*the great movement of apostasy*"? (1910). This makes it impossible for such a force not to know what it is doing, or to maintain that it is seriously interested in the religious well-being of mankind. The use of pretexts, as the Holy Father charges the Movement with practising, shows that the deception is deliberate, and that the leaders are aiming for something different: in fact quite the opposite of what the deceived are made to believe.

As we will see progressively better, when the story of this deception unfolds, there is ample evidence to make the charge stick, that the *real* aims and objectives of this 'great Movement of Apostasy' (to give this drive for the one-world 'religion' its real name) are global *political power*, or *world dominance*, as St. John already clearly foretold us in his Book of Revelation. Pope St. Pius X underscored these Divine predictions by pointing out that this antichurch would bring back to the world "the reign of legalised cunning, and brute force, and the oppression of the weak, and of all those who toil and suffer". (1910). We recognise these, not as religious objectives, but for what they really are: the exact aims and methods of communism. That such an anti-church, masquerading as a true one, would be intolerant of the true Catholic Church and would strive for its extinction, is inevitable. True Catholicism, as distinct from its modernistic and teilhardian counterfeit, does not fit with Communism and Syncretism as it is intolerant of any form of falsehood and error in its teaching. Its very nature is to overcome deception, in fierce resistance to lies and deceit. The Catholic Church's first and foremost instinct is to uphold and defend Revealed Truth. *It is the very nature and instinct of the 'church of darkness' to withhold and suppress it.*

If Syncretism, according to the definition of one of its innumerable apologists, is *"the intent of its advocates to create a single world religion, by taking the BEST ELEMENTS from each religion, and fusing them into one, or picking out what is UNIQUE in the different faiths, and making one religion out of them, which would be universally acceptable since it would contain (vital) elements of every religion."* (Dr. Donald Bishop, Ph D, Dept of Philosophy, Washington State University, in the 1970 Autumn edition of *World Faiths*),

then no one has yet seen that, over the last 150-odd years, the Syncretists have taken *THE BEST* out of Catholicism, or those things, which make Catholicism *VITAL* and *UNIQUE*. The glaring absence of any love of the Syncretists for what is *vital*, *unique*, and *the best* in Catholicism, gives the lie to any claim 'that the organisers of the world church are objective and sincere'; which is the same as saying that they try to deceive.

Being a 'Movement of Apostasy', it is only of late that the Syncretists have welcomed with open arms what teilhardian 'catholics' have brought in as their share in the great apostasy, but only because the modernistic heresies these diseased catholics carried with them *were already part and parcel of the Brotherhood's outfit and composition anyhow!*

It is time we have a good look at some of the evidence which is piling up in the Great Movement's literature. The profoundly distressing feature of it all is, that all this evidence, like uncollected garbage, is spilling out over a world redeemed by the Precious Blood of the Lamb of God, and the 'masterminds' are fooling around with property bought and paid for by the Sufferings and Death of the Son of the Blessed Virgin Mary ....

A. The New Order

As will come to light soon, this Great Movement of Apostasy is made up of a bewildering assortment of bodies, which, like veritable parasites, crawl and feast on the moribund remains of the European Christian Civilisation, which has slowly and agonisingly starved itself to death by cutting off, one by one, the many life-supporting systems which had sustained it so successfully for a thousand years.

When an old regime is in its final throes, a new order is ready to finish it off and take its place. Since it is the *Christian* European Civilisation which is coming to an end, we can be sure of one thing: whatever it is that is instrumental in bringing it to a close in order to replace it, it will never be *christian!* It will not even be truly *religious*, no matter how hard it tries to give that impression ... Hence the origin of deception.

With this set-up, History has provided us with all the trappings of a classical Greek drama:

- A global intrigue, wishing to give the impression of being invincible and to be considered an important part of the reality of our times.
- A force, which is presenting itself as a 'religious movement', but which in reality is after political power.
- A one-world 'church' in preparation for one-world control.

- And, as St. John puts it, '*a second beast*', making out to be concerned with the unity Christ willed, thus pretending '*to look like the Lamb*', but meanwhile doing everything in its power to achieve a totally different unity: the unification of the world under the tyranny of '*the first beast*', and thus '*speaking like the Dragon ...*' (Rev.13:11-17.)

In order to get some idea of the seeming complexity of the present-day religio-syncretist movement, here are some of the names of the more important bodies associated with it. The information is supplied by John Cotter in his informative little book: *A Study in Syncretism.*

"The new *World Faith Synthesis* to replace all religions, especially Christianity, which *Synthesis* is usually referred to as WORLD or UNIVERSAL BROTHERHOOD, has for many years been the focus of attention and the sole centre of activity of such groups as: *Baha'is,*

the Theosophists,
the Vedanta,
the World Congress of Faiths,
the World Brotherhood of Faiths,
the World Fellowship of Faiths,
the World Alliance for International Friendship through Religion,
the World Spiritual Council,
the World Spiritual Communist Congress(!),
Sufism,

Union for the Study of the Great Religions,

Divine Life Society,

Subud,

Universal Golden Rule Crusade,

Golden Rule Spiritual United Nations Crusade,

Unity,

The Unitarians,

The World Council of Churches,

The National Council of Churches.

All of these are offshoots of the UNIVERSAL BROTHER-HOOD MOVEMENT *before 1924!* Members of this movement were / are:

The Universal Brotherhood (Paris, 1923),

Neugeist Bund (Germany, 1922),

International Fellowship (India, 1922),

The League of Neighbours (America, 1920, by members of the
     World Jewish Congress),

the Church Peace Union (America, 1914),

the Union of East and West (London, 1910),

the Union of International Associations (Continent, 1910),

the International New life Fellowship (1906),

and the Big Daddy of them all:

the World Parliament of Religions,

held in Chicago in 1893, and of which the President of *the London Buddhist Society* said in 1950 at the World Congress of Faiths: 'The effect of this pioneer effort in religious synthesis has never died'. How right he was …"

We can add to all of this the many *Teilhard de Chardin Institutes, Associations, Congresses and Fellowships*, which all have their roots deep in the same rosicrucian mumbo-jumbo and pseudo-scientific clap-trap as all the others, and whose only claim to fame is to create the pretence that the Catholic Church Herself has somehow gone over to the ideas of 'the second beast'.

Running through this perplexing proliferation, as an unmistakable 'Red Thread', scarlet with the blood of countless Martyrs, is the word and reality of "*Brotherhood*". A unifying concept, betraying the presence of a unifying will, and held aloft by an unseen hand mailed by an iron glove …. It is this ugly and fearsome reality which forced St. John to refer to it, in the 13th chapter of the *Book of Revelation*, as "the second beast", and which forces us to investigate very closely how the holy author could predict in the Holy Spirit: "… that it would do everything in its power to subjugate the world to the tyranny of the First Beast". To verify, in other words, that, when all is said and done, the second beast is nothing but the first beast under a different and very misleading appearance….

It is not difficult to show, even from the far from complete list printed above, that it was the intention of the Brotherhood that the original meaning by which it wished to be known publicly *was the one of a* Religious Fraternity, with a respectable image of a kind of earnest endeavour to comply with Christ's wish "that all should be one". (In 'Revelation parlance' this translates: "that it was the wish of the first beast to be universally known as an entity 'that looked like the lamb'". But unfortunately, every time 'the Brothers' open their mouths, as is the case with every modernist priest or teilhardian nun, who even more 'look like the Lamb': 'they sound like the Dragon'.)

Is it possible to sustain that this 'religious' beginning is fraudulent? That it only served as a cloak to hide the real identity? And is it further possible to ascertain the nature of that 'real' identity? And so to substantiate St. John's claim: "that the movement that wished to be known as 'looking like the Lamb', did nevertheless everything in its power to subjugate the world to the tyranny of the first beast, 'Satan's most powerful seed'? What about the more recent meanings of 'the Brotherhood'?

At this stage of our narrative we are clearly saddled with a dual task:

(i) to give evidence that 'the Brotherhood' has assumed a more recent *political* identity, different from the *religious* one originally portrayed, [**B**]; and

(ii) to uncover 'the half-way mark': meetings and congresses where there is a quite brutal attempt to *publicly* enforce the acceptance of the political meaning, without drawing attention to the fact that the religious meaning has been dropped, as if such a shift is the most normal thing in the world to do ..., [**C**]

If this evidence can be produced, then THE BROTHERHOOD has laid itself wide open to a charge of subversion, fraud and deceit, and will then carry all the earmarks, whereby St. John has foretold and described to us its (future) dual existence. Let us see what we can come to light with.

B. The Shift in Identity

"The Citadel will be stormed under the banners of Liberty and Democracy. And once the <u>apparatus of power</u> is in the hands of '<u>The Brotherhood</u>', all opposition, all contrary opinion must be punished by death to extinction. Democracy is but a tool to be used and afterwards broken; Liberty but a sentimental folly unworthy of the logician. The absolute rule <u>of a self-chosen priesthood</u> (!), according to the dogmas it has learned by rote, is to be imposed <u>upon mankind</u> without mitigation, progressively forever. All this set out in prosy textbooks, but written also in blood in the history of several powerful nations, is the Communists' faith and purpose."

Clear language, as can be expected from its author, none other than the late great Winston Churchill, from his book *Great Contemporaries*, in an essay dealing with Leon Trotsky, p. 168-9.

But if this is to be dismissed as a testimony of an outsider, however alerted we may be by it, we cannot depend on it in isolation.

"I can tell you that 'The Brotherhood' exists, but I cannot tell you if it numbers a hundred members, or ten million. From your personal knowledge you will never be able to say that it numbers even as many as a dozen … The Brotherhood cannot be wiped out, because it is not an organisation in the ordinary sense …"

These words were spoken by "O'Brien", a 'man of mysteriously high rank in the inner party', a fictitious figure in Orwell's great book *1984*.   George Orwell is anything but fictitious! A King's scholar in Britain's top-notch Eton College, he was an important British socialist who turned decisively anti-communist after serving for one year on the communist side in the Spanish Civil War. And so 'O'Brien's message' may be taken as a piece of information from a brilliant man who was a semi-insider.

"Comrade Deputies, on the instruction of the Central Committee of the CPSU and the <u>Council of Elders</u>, I wish to propose as Chairman of the Council of Ministers of the Soviet Socialist Republics Comrade Nikolai Alexandrovitch Bulganin."

If the two previous testimonies could be ignored 'as not coming from the inside', this accusation could hardly be levelled at the last one, as it is the official beginning of the quoted speech, which deputy N. S. Khrushchev gave, early in February, 1955.   The term *'Council of Elders'* attracted world-wide attention, as it is one of the customary ways of referring to 'The Brotherhood', supposedly an organisation concerned with unity in religion … e.g. the late Lord Beaverbrook's influential London 'Daily Express' in its number of February 9 stated: "Such a council has never been mentioned before".   Whatever it is, it must have been powerful enough to dictate instructions to 'dictator Khrushchev' about who should be made Prime Minister of the Soviet Union.

According to these initial testimonies, the 'Brotherhood', through its leaders, the Council of Elders, is after political power, as distinct from its earlier image of being only a 'Brotherhood' of religious unification.   Since there is no trace of evidence to be found anywhere of a rival 'Brotherhood' having set itself up for the acquisition of *political* power, as distinct from an original 'Brotherhood' whose only aim was the religious unification of the world, we are forced to accept not only that it is the same 'Brotherhood' speaking through the two appearances, but even more so that *the later manifestation of the political 'Brotherhood' is the only and real existence of this power group*, and that all the original 'concern' for religious unity was nothing but a front: a means to deceit, to make itself accepted and popular as a world body and global organisation. And it is this fearsome power group, which wishes to fill the vacuum, left by the eclipse of the European Christian Civilisation.

C. Evidence for a "Change in Mid-Stream" Proposed as an Accomplished Fact in the Brotherhood's Power Struggle

After the earlier glimpses of a dual character of 'the Brotherhood', the so-called *'religious'* World Congresses continued, but they took on more and more of a *political* nature, especially after the early 1970's, as if by then this transition from one to the other had been universally accepted as an accomplished fact, a natural development. We will have a brief look at a couple of the more glaring examples of this phenomenon. After that we will have to return, in the second half of this chapter, to a more detailed study of where exactly, and how, this blatant switch from 'religious' to 'political' actually took place.

1. "By far the most important syncretist meeting in recent years was held in Kyoto, near Tokyo, Japan, from October 16-22, 1970. Its official title was:

"The First World Conference of Religion for Peace"

It is to be understood that neither such a conference nor its far-reaching aims could be realised without considerable spade work at lower national as well as higher international levels. The mind simply boggles if one considers the amount of coordination and preparatory work done, and the amount of money spent on its preparation. It was the first of its kind where the bold transition from 'religion' to 'politics' was to be presented and accepted on a world-scale. That alone, as one can appreciate, requires considerable ground work in all countries. (It is sad, but true, that the late Card. John Wright of the U.S.A. played some role in the founding of this very sinister syncretist movement.)

Catholics from 17 nations made up the largest single group ...

In his opening address, the Conference President, *the Catholic Archbishop of New Delhi, Angelo Fernandes,* (who was to be President again of the 2nd World Congress in 1974, in Louvain, Belgium, and was prominent at the 3rd Congress in 1979, at Princeton, U.S.A.), addressing more than 1600 hundred delegates, called for the formation of a WORLD PARLIAMENT OF RELIGION, which should have "the independence and impartiality of a judiciary body" and which should act "unhesitatingly and fearlessly ...". If we consider that this 1st Conference (which obviously was meant to set the tone and the pace and the direction of all the ones to follow) dealt exclusively *with non-religious matters,* such as 'disarmament', 'human rights', 'human development' (!), then, in the mind of the ORGANISING BROTHERHOOD, the 'Parliament of Religions' was to be set up *for political and economic purposes.*

"Conceived a mere decade ago by 4 American clergymen (!), the world conference now under way culminated 10 years of grad-

ual and painstaking effort in world-wide ecumenism and preparatory gatherings." (From *Western Catholic Reporter*, Canada.)

Most of this 'painstaking effort' was spent in making sure that
only suitable delegates would be invited, as came out even more
patently in the convening of the 2nd World Congress in Louvain,
1974.

"In Kyoto, the World Council of Churches was represented by
its General Secretary, Dr. Carson Blake. Of Blake's Kyoto speech,
Sir Muhammad Zafrulla Kahn, President of the International
Court of Justice in The Hague, Holland, ex-foreign minister of Pa-
kistan and President of the 17th session of the United Nations, said:
'Dr. Blake did not stress any single value which I, as a Muslim,
could not wholly endorse'."

(From *World Faiths*, Summer, 1971.)

This, of course, stands to reason. Gone was all the talk about
'Jesus Christ, our Lord and Saviour'. Here at Kyoto the WCC sat
down on terms with absolute equality with every religious shade
under the sun *because there simply was no longer any talk about
religion* … We can be certain, then, that if 'The Brotherhood' sees
fit to create a 'parliament of religion', it will be wholly at the service
of its *political* ends. Since the call for it came from a *political* gathering: at Kyoto in 1970.

It is impossible not to think here of 'The World Parliament of
Religion' of Chicago, 1893, where some 300 delegates attended
portions of this mammoth 17 day conference, coinciding with a
September World Fair. The Archbishop of Canterbury declined an
invitation saying that Christianity was the only true religion and
that participants implied that the other religions were equal to

Christianity. Even stronger condemnations came from other Christian quarters. One missionary called it 'a betrayal of Christ'.

2.   If Chicago of 1893 must be seen as the beginning of an organised betrayal of Christ by some Christian leaders, and Kyoto of 1970 must equally be viewed as the beginning of an organised betrayal of Christ by some *Catholic* leaders, then the 2nd *World Conference of Religion for Peace*, held at the 'catholic' university of Louvain, Belgium, from August 28 – September 3, was an unconditional capitulation to 'The Brotherhood'.

The delegates, 350 or so, the 'christians', even including the puppets from behind the Iron Curtain, heavily outnumbered and outvoted, even assuming they were united in defence of basic Christian beliefs, which they were not, were hand-picked from the ultra-left.

The '*Preliminary Studies for Background Information*' supplied to the delegates, are the pre-set policies of 'The Brotherhood'. And 'Woe' to the delegate who departs one iota from them! The delegates are there to lend the prestige of their name *not to formulate policy!* This is done beforehand in the intervening time between two congresses.

[Even the then Canadian Prime Minister, Pierre Trudeau, an ardent supporter and member of 'The Club of Rome' (another tentacle of 'The Brotherhood'), found this same procedure irksome at the 'Club of Rome' meeting he attended in Austria in February, 1974. From the Toronto *Star*, August 17, 1974.]

The Louvain Program:

(1) Disarmament and Security.
(2) Economic Development and Human Liberation.
(3) Human Rights and Fundamental Freedoms.
(4) Environment and Survival.

It is obvious from this blatantly 'party-line' program that for the majority of mankind *religion* has become synonymous with *economics and politics*, exactly as 'The Brotherhood' intended *right from the start.* [Remember St. John? The First Beast (political and economic enslavement) IS the Second Beast, appearing in the travesty of a 'religious' garb.] Salvation from Sin and Hell has been replaced by Liberation from any form of religion!

Yes, for 'The Brotherhood', it must have been worth the effort and patience. Already, as we know, the World Council of Churches has earmarked, through its various National Council of Churches, as "*maverick churches*" any Church (and we all know whom they mean as that one) that does not go along with this brand of ecumenism, syncretism and 'religion'; who refuses to give up its own Creed and identity. (See *The Coming World Church*, Back to the Bible Publication, Lincoln, Nebraska, 1963, p. 16-17.) The *Parliament of Religions* will have to deal with this type of deviation and revisionism "unhesitatingly and fearlessly" according to the opening speech *by a Catholic Archbishop* who was President of the 1st Conference in Kyoto. What a weapon in the hands of future persecutors of the Catholic Church! Presented to them by apostate Catholics themselves … For we must never forget that the name Pope St. Pius X gave to the formation of this one-world 'church of darkness' was "the great movement of apostasy …".

II

Chapter Interlude

We are now very close to the second part of this chapter on DECEPTION: an investigation into what is known about the *transition* from the earlier appearance of a religion-orientated movement to its present-day stunning climax; from a 'brotherhood' in religious fraternity to 'The Brotherhood' behind political one-world dictatorship.

But first, since evil-doers and plotters are *scattering in the wind*, because they are not *collecting* with Christ, no matter how successful they may appear to be, it is very instructive and consoling to be shown a glimpse of how *the little Eucharistic Lamb*, and not the 'Brotherhood', is in charge of the direction of world events. Totally unbeknown to the arch-plotters, for they cannot attend to every detail, their Louvain meeting gave away a clue so important as to reveal the true nature of that gathering already made known by Our Lord *more than 150 years previously!* The revealing detail is central to the whole message of the 'World Conference for Religion and Peace', and was expressed in the first of its Louvain meetings in these words:

"We appeal to the religious communities of the world to inculcate the attitude of PLANETARY citizenship, the sense of our human solidarity (in the redeeming Blood of Our Saviour? Or in the Fatherhood of God? No,) in the just sharing of the food, the energy and all the *material* necessities of existence …". (From 'The

Louvain Declaration', in the *Catholic Register*, Toronto, September 21, 1974.)

Remember, this is a 'World Conference on RELIGION', but the jargon is so obviously 'of this world', for the formation of a one-world economic and political order, with no longer any thought towards 'citizenship in the Kingdom of Heaven' or in the 'City of God', that Our Lord, with the unsuspected use made here of this word "*planetary*" alone, has revealed for us His Divine Judgement on these matters, as a guide for our own thinking after careful study.

In a book by Fr. K. E. Schmoeger, CSsR, of which the German original received an Imprimatur in 1867, and the French translation an Imprimatur in 1868, (the latter Imprimatur rather unique, as the French translation was made by no other than the Vicar General of the Cathedral of Versailles) we read the following:

September 12, 1820. *"I saw a fantastic, odd-looking 'church' being built. The choir was in 3 parts and under it was a deep vault full of fog. I saw no Angel helping in the construction, but numbers of the most VIOLENT PLANETARY spirits dragging all sorts of things into the vault, where persons in little ecclesiastical mantles received them and deposited them in their various places. Nothing was brought from Above: all came from the earth and the dark region, and all was built up by planetary spirits. I saw an enormous number of instruments brought into the 'church' and many persons, even children, had different tools, as if trying to make something; but all was obscure, absurd, DEAD. Division and destruction reigned everywhere. I saw that many of the instruments, such as spears and darts, were meant to be used against the Living Church. Everyone dragged in something different …*

The men in the little mantles brought wood to the steps of the pulpit to make fire. (Listen to this!) *They puffed and blew and laboured hard, but the fire would not burn: all they produced was smoke and fumes. Then they broke a hole in the roof and ran up a pipe, but the smoke would not rise and the whole place became black and suffocating. ALL IN THIS 'CHURCH' BELONG TO THE EARTH. All was dead, the work of human skill, a 'church' of the latest style, a 'church' of man's invention like the new heterodox 'church' in Rome."*

November 12, 1820. *"I passed over a dark, cold country to a large city, and I saw again the great odd-looking 'church' with nothing holy about it AND INNUMERABLE PLANETARY SPIRITS labouring at it. I saw a 'spirit' on high drawing lines and tracing figures, and down below the design, the plan, immediately carried out. I saw the influence of the proud, planetary spirits in their relation with the building extended TO EVEN THE MOST DISTANT PLACES. All the steps deemed necessary or useful to the construction and maintenance of the 'church' were taken IN THE MOST REMOTE COUNTRIES, and men and things, doctrines and opinions contributed thereto. The whole picture was coloured with intense selfishness, presumption and VIOLENCE. I saw not a single Angel or Saint helping in the work. Far away in the background I saw the throne of a savage nation and a figure saying in mocking terms: 'Build it as solidly as you please, we shall overturn it!'."*

(From the *Life of the Ven. Servant of God, Anna Catharina EMMERICH*. English translation by Maria Regina Guild, 1885 and 1903, pp.282-284.)

It is noteworthy, in context, to be told that His Holiness Pope Pius IX *ordered* the Italian translation to be made from the advanced proof-sheets of the German text.

There is a welter of information about our times to be gleaned from this extra-ordinary life, and I am certain that we would render ourselves a great service in our tribulations, so well understood and foreseen by this wonderful servant of God, if we prayed *"that she may be canonised BY our times for all she has done and suffered FOR our times ..."*. For it appears that, 160 years ago, the Venerable Anna Catharina Emmerich had a far clearer understanding of what was going on in our times than many of our ecclesiastical dignitaries have today. That this is not surprising is made very clear by her in subsequent sections of her fascinating life-story.

III

The Stages of the Deception

Enlightened by the foregoing, we will have no trouble finishing off the jig-saw puzzle. The 'Brotherhood' for a One-World dictatorship was <u>first</u> known also as 'The Illuminati', 'The Council of Elders', 'The Martinists' (to which the late Pierre Teilhard de Chardin belonged), etc. [The 'First Beast', the *political* tyranny in the *Book of Revelation*, ch. 13, of St. John.] To cash in on the deep-rooted hunger in a spiritually starved humanity for communion with God, 'THEY' decided not only to work 'through the secular': the International Bankers, the Council of Foreign Relations, the Institute of Pacific Relations, the tax-exempt Foundations, the United Nations, the Club of Rome, the secular press, the humanist universities, the political parties, but to work also 'through the sacred': through 'religion', creating a fraternity of all religions, the World Council of Churches, the National Council of Churches, [the odd-looking 'church of darkness' in the visions of Anna Catharina Emmerich], and through the teilhardian, modernist 'church', masquerading as a true interpretation of Catholicism, [the other, newfangled, heterodox 'church' she described]. This was their second arm, or, to give 20th century confirmation to St. John, the 'Second Beast'. Although in time it appeared *second*, in the public eye it appeared as The Brotherhood's first pathway, but with the unwavering aim to achieve its first objective: a one-world dictatorship. What could give more confirmation to the accuracy of the Revelations of St. John, who told us that 'a religious-looking evil': 'looking like the Lamb, but speaking like the Dragon', would do everything in its power to subjugate the world 'to the First Beast': a politically-minded evil? According to St. John, then, the vision of and preparation for a socio-political one-world dictatorship came first, but it created the one-world 'church' as its second arm, making out as if the religious unity of mankind grew spontaneously first in preparation of a longed-for political unity.

Herein lies the deceit. For, as we have seen from the Louvain meeting, there really is no longer any religion, not even any talk about it! Careful planning, selective choice of suitable 'delegates', and an iron fist of coercion and ruthless regimentation, have all been used to replace the Holy Spirit to smooth the way for the merger of the socio-political 'Brotherhood' with the 'religious' one, and to keep the two wedded together forever. And now that the Second Beast, the one-world 'church of darkness', has openly and distinctly fused with the socio-political beast, there is no longer any need for pretence, only force and caution.

But somewhere along the line there must have occurred a sub-tle (?) <u>transition</u>, where the deceit was at its peak, and where people for the first time accepted the POLITICAL ends of the 'Brother-hood' as the RELIGIOUS ones. If that period of transition can be found, then the aims and reasons for the deceit will be laid bare and become very simple indeed. And then the full force of St. John's prediction will be felt by mankind: when the 'religious-looking Beast' will do everything in its power to crush humanity under the global tyranny of Antichrist. When so-called 'religion' will assume and enforce 'politics'…

There are several pieces left over to complete the picture on the jig-saw puzzle:

> (1) "If <u>world unity</u> is to be attained, it must be through In-ternational Communism, which can only be arrived at by the slogan: 'Banish God from the skies, and capital-ists from the earth'. Then, and only then, will there ex-ist a complete <u>Fellowship of Faiths</u>."

This impossible and untenable contradiction was seriously propounded by (don't laugh) Bishop William Montgomery Brown, spokesman for the 'World Fellowship of Faiths', at their First World Congress, Chicago, 1933. What does it say?

"*World Unity*". This is a political concept.

"*International Communism*" is at best a politico-economic system, and at worst an arch-enemy of freedom and religion.

"*Banish God from the skies*" is a blasphemous anti-religious concept, and a totally futile one at that.

"*and (banish) capitalists from the earth*" is a murderous anti-social concept.

And this blatantly *political, anti-religious and anti-God* program is pompously and seriously being advocated by a *bishop*, a man-of-God, as the sole condition for the final establishment of a purely *religious* reality: the 'Fellowship of Faiths'. But this global 'religion' must be completely devoid of God, since He ought to be banished. So, this bishop's religious concept of 'faith' is a fraudulent one! What else is this type of 'world faith' but naked politics?

What this piece of nonsense DOES contain, then, is *a complete identification of the political 'Brotherhood' with the so-called 'religious Brotherhood'. A fusion of the First Beast and the Second Beast.* But worst of all: it did not cause a ripple. If delegates can swallow that, they can swallow anything from then on. They had obviously accepted it as a fact-of-life that it was in their best interest to swallow this fusion of a 'one-world religion' with one-world politics.

If ever a man 'looks like the Lamb', it is a bishop. If ever a bishop 'spoke like the Dragon' it was this one, and the many ones like him …

(2) "Communism, on the other hand, can be regarded as a serious candidate for the title of a WORLD RELIGION."

These words were uttered by Sir Julian HUXLEY in the Presidential Address to the *First International Congress on Humanism*, Amsterdam, 1952. Apparently words can be made to mean anything. The 'slogan' contains the same fusion of unacceptable contraries as in (1) above, with the same identification of political and 'religious' slavery and the same inevitable result *that it was accepted!*

No wonder St. John could predict some 2000 years ago that one day "the whole world would run after the beast". This is the type of crooked thinking that will hail 'the Beast', and if a one World Congress accepts it, a subsequent World Congress is not going to reject it, if both are organised *by the same organisation: the same 'Brotherhood'* …

(3) "1951 saw yet another one of those 'world' congresses; this time the *World Spiritual Communist Congress*, organised by the VEDANTA Movement and convened in London. The aim was to air before the world a couple of articles of faith of this VEDANTA group:"

    (i)   that it stood for the spiritual and material unity of all mankind, and that it was fully convinced that *'spiritual communism'* is the fullest expression of Universal Brotherhood (!), and

    (ii) that it called for the development of the United Nations into a World Federal Government, "with the socialisation of the means of production, distribution and exchange *without compensation!* As the basis of a sound economic system …".

The key-word in this whole mesmerising mish-mash is once again "planetary citizenship". Since it is the key-word, God seized on it and showed Anna Catharina EMMERICH what exactly 'building a new religion for political purposes' really involved. It is instructive to learn from contemporary literature how the coining of the word and the idea, as expressed in the above: '*spiritual communism*', has fused the two appearances of 'the Beast'. This explains why all those who are stubborn enough to try to keep the two sides of the one coin separate are deluding themselves, and will find themselves helplessly dragged along the road as 'fellow travellers'. It is naive to maintain that it is possible to accept only one side of the coin, e.g. to go along with political idea of, say, 'one-world week', whilst trying to ignore the other side, dissociating oneself from the religious implications. It mystifies Catholics, including priests and bishops, who are as unfamiliar with the Catholic Church's Social Teaching as they are with contemporary deception-literature, why this concept of 'planetary citizenship' is only vaguely disquieting and seems harmless enough in this age of jets and computers.

They fail to grasp that in the future many Catholics are going to be liquidated, ostensibly for rejecting the political unity symbolised by 'planetary citizenship'; but in reality they will be *martyred*, because in the Supernatural Light of their Catholic Faith, they clearly see they are requested by God *to reject the 'religious' side of the same coin!* The world will be told that they deserve annihilation because they are opposed to the 'political unity' represented by the image of the First Beast, stamped on one side of the coin; but in reality they will be crucified for their Faith which clearly tells them that it is impossible to accept the political tyranny without <u>aposta-</u> <u>sy</u>. Without adoring the Beast in its temple: the one-world 'church of darkness', created by the Second Beast and stamped on the reverse side of the same coin...

We do not have to look very far to find out where this diabolical master stroke of genius comes from: this creation of a dual system, which allows the persecution of people for their Supernatural Faith whilst proclaiming to all the world their rejection of the religious unity of the world makes them betrayers of the political unity of mankind, *and thus its number one enemy.* Even if they never opened their mouth against the political and economic slavery under Antichrist: because of their rejection of his 'religious' unity of mankind, they will still become *political* prisoners, and they will be liquidated for their 'crimes' against the political unity of mankind, deprived of the honour and consolation of dying for their Faith ...

Far fetched? Read on!

(4) "The BAHA'I revelation is the spirit of the age. It is the essence of all the highest ideals of this century. The Baha'i cause is an inclusive movement; the teachings of all religions and societies are found there. Christians, Jews, Buddhists, Mohammedans, Zoroastrians, Theosophists, Freemasons, Spiritists, etc., find their highest aims in this cause.

Socialists and philosophers find their theories fully developed in this revelation."

This boast came from the pen of one ABDU'L-BAHA, son of the self-appointed founder of the Baha'i faith. This faith is so close to the ideas of 'The Brotherhood', and is followed by so many millions around the world, who not only know nothing about this 'faith' or its origin, but would quite readily believe that it is an expression of their own vague religious convictions, that ever since the origins of it in the middle of last century, it had the ideal chameleon properties for any *political* organisation wanting to dominate the world through *'religion'*.

Three things stand out:

(i) Must we repeat it? Baha'i policy is identical with official communist policy as laid down by Stalin and Lenin;

(ii) the Baha'i were the first to clamour for a world police force *and for world citizenship*. BAHA'U'LLAH, the founder, has stated:

"It is not for him to pride himself who loveth his own country but rather for him who loveth the whole world." (From *World Faiths*, Summer, 1977.)

And:

"The earth is but one country, and mankind its citizens ...".

(iii) The enforced 'unity' of all religions is foreshadowed by mentioning several by name, which are portrayed as having already benefitted from it....

If 'Planetary Citizenship' is still being portrayed as an article of 'religious faith' (which, as already stated, blends in easily with other religions' beliefs), and we hear Communists and their fellow-travellers claiming an identical ideology *for political purposes*, cashing in on the aspirations of the millions who see nothing wrong in it, then we may start to appreciate *that 'PLANETARY CITIZEN-SHIP' is the door through which both the First and Second Beast have access to minds where they have no business.*

People open to this idea will readily read up on whatever literature is available on the subject, and so they become uncritical and easy prey for other deceptions formulated as 'reasonable' policies and decisions, taken by all those 'inter-faith' meetings.

Finally:

(5) "Under Communism, humanity will reach the time when national distinctions and national languages will disappear, and a merging of the nations will come about." [From *Bourgeois Nations and Socialist Nations.* Foreign Language Publishing House. Moscow, 1954.]"

And:

(6) "The aim of Socialism is the elimination of the fragmentation of humanity in petty states and the individualism of

nations. Not only the coming closer together of nations, but there merger or fusion." (Lenin, 1916.) [From *Time*, September 20, 1968.]."

Here, then, we have the Communist version of 'Planetary Citizenship' and its ultimate objectives. Since Baha'i policy is indistinguishable from it, whoever tries to follow a 'religious' ideal in this area, or vice versa, accepting a political ideal without the obvious 'religious' overlayers, is deluding himself since the so-called 'religious' path to planetary citizenship is fused with the Communist one, as God revealed to Anna Catharina EMMERICH.

IV

Conclusion

Australian Catholics seem irrevocably wedded to these 'ideals' through the thoughtless and hasty EPISCOPAL CONFERENCE decision to give unqualified support to *One-World Week*, sponsored almost exclusively by the Australian Council of Churches. Since it is a foregone conclusion that this decision will not be reversed, the KEY-IDEA has now not only been adopted by the bishops at large, but has been implanted as a trigger, into the minds of millions of others as an innocent enterprise. Through this door untold other equally seemingly innocuous ideas will penetrate into the subconscious minds of many Catholics, by which gradual dissociation from authentic Catholic Teaching will be achieved.

Since PLANETARY CITIZENSHIP and the ONE-WORLD MOVEMENTS are so obviously *political*, with barely a flavour of religion left in them, (which, as we know, was a totally false 'religion' anyhow) it is distressing that later on Catholics will have to stand up and dissociate themselves from these seemingly petty, but for 'The Beast' important POLITICAL issues, because of the cast-iron condition attached to them: *that all 'planetary citizens'* (the First Beast, the political side of the one coin) *have one 'planetary religion'*, (the Second Beast, the 'religious' side of the coin. Same coin: same Beast.) And this stipulation makes the whole idea of 'planetary citizenship' anything but innocent! This unacceptable clause makes it mandatory to Catholics and other sincere Christians to reject it. Their rejection of apostasy will be played down, their opposition to political unity will be implied, and maximised, and will be much better understood and accepted by the masses, 'since the whole world will run after the Beast …'.

"Nothing can stop the advent and appearance of the ultimate physical form …" (Mrs. Bailey, 1933.)

Granted. But *SOMEBODY* can. The One to whom it is given 'to crush the serpent's head: him, and his seed'.

It is time we turned to Her.

Chapter Two

Not Deceived

There are several reasons why the important matters set out in the previous chapter fail to impress a great majority of Catholics nowadays.

For one, "things are never eaten as hot as they are served". It is human to dismiss as exaggerated that which is not obvious to many. When the time comes, things will have cooled down a little, and we will deal with the situation as best we can.

Secondly, to those not affected by it, any discussion on 'deception' and 'conspiracies' is boring. We put them aside for the time being, to get absorbed in everyday living, 'leaving the future to God …'.

Lastly, these abstruse things are really only clearly perceived in the Supernatural Light of Catholic Faith, and – sad but true – there are, in our times, only too many who have neglected this priceless gift from God, and who no longer can tell the difference between Catholic Faith and any other faith. How would they know, if they have lost their Catholic Faith? Are changing it? Or are in the process of losing it? And in the ensuing darkness of mind they fail to see *that this loss of Catholic Faith* is precisely the purpose of the total war, declared by the enemy on the Catholic Church. And for this, they have only themselves to blame, for the Church knew of the attack and supplied us with strategies and remedies in plenty of time.

So, whatever reason is given for non-involvement: on closer scrutiny we will always discover at the bottom of it some erosion of Catholic Faith, and thereby some success of the enemy's strategy. For all Catholics are automatically involved simply because they are in the possession of that rare and priceless pearl: the one and only thing the enemy-in-the-know wants to relieve them of: their Catholic Faith …

Take e.g. the very plausible answer to (2) above: 'leaving the future to God …'. 'Futures' are shaped and prepared by 'presents'. If a strong measure of Catholic Faith, by their own admission is necessary later, then it must be prepared for now! If they want God to look after their future, if they need Divine Assistance in the future, then they must lay the foundations for that assistance now. But are they doing that by getting engrossed in everyday living? Have a look at the enemy himself. Just as the enemy is preparing NOW for a take-over LATER, taking *appropriate* steps without allowing himself to get sidetracked by the pleasures and cares of this world, so a strong resistance later must be appropriately prepared for now. There are many 'foolish virgins' around who neglect to take an adequate supply of oil with them now for later use and who leave it too late to do anything about it! The 5 originals in the Gospel too 'left the future to God', but in the parable which contains Divine Wisdom, God did not supply them with the oil they lacked, and which they refused to acquire in the appropriate time of preparation …

These considerations, then, make the subject-matter of the previous chapter extremely important for a number of reasons.

Firstly, forewarned is forearmed. If so far one has managed to steer clear from any attempt at deception the Evil one had in mind for one's particular circumstances, thank God, but beware. The enemy is very persistent and clever. It is really one who is only kept at bay by fasting and prayer. (Our Lord, Our Lady at Fatima!) There will always be another day with another design.

Moreover, we would never think our fellow man in mortal danger, (and consequently would not think it necessary to come to his aid), if we ourselves would be totally ignorant of the danger.

Next, if we wish to help our fellow man to get himself disentangled from the stranglehold of the enemy, we need to be acquainted with the latter's tactics and strategies, which presupposes some study in depth.

Finally, many catholics are there, in the company of deceit and subversion *because they want to be there!* Which means that, if we want to follow Our Lord's example Who did not leave us in the powers of darkness, we will not only have to do battle with the enemy, *but with the ignorance of the victims as well.* All this demands some knowledge of the climate of deception in which we live, and in which we have to work out our own as well as our brothers' salvation.

What the subject-matter of the first chapter should have brought home to us very forcefully is, that there must be a staggering amount of people in the Christian camp, who profess to believe in Jesus Christ, yet are part and parcel of the network of deception; actively engaged in its soul-destroying mission. This raises by necessity grave doubts in the minds of onlookers: 'Do these self-professed christians really believe in Jesus Christ as the Son of God,

Who has a prior claim on their fidelity *in adhering to the authentic Spirit of His Revelation?*' And further – and even more so in the case of catholic participants in the global work of THE BROTHERHOOD: 'Do these people seriously believe, that Our Lord and Saviour left behind on earth an Authority to preserve the authentic interpretation of that Revelation, which Authority must bind in conscience if it is to perform its saving function?'

The thrust of the question can bluntly be put like this:

'If a public proclaiming of Christ, yes, even a public profession in Christ, did not prevent the existence of the most divergent and even contradictory streams in Christianity, and did not guard many against deception and delusion, then what will?'

To find the answer, we will have to look to the Catholic Church for guidance.

I

The Catholic Church's Teaching on Faith

CATHOLIC FAITH is different from any other faith on earth. That makes Catholic Faith unique. It is the only Faith on earth of which the acts of Faith are being done in submission, in obedience and humility to the teachings of the Catholic Church. Many people believe in God for whatever reason; a Catholic believes in God *because the Catholic Church teaches him there is a Trinity in God*. Many people who *profess* to believe in Jesus Christ, also seem to claim that they can please themselves if they believe in His Divinity or not. A Catholic believes in the Divinity of Christ, because the

Catholic Church teaches him that Christ is the Second Person of the Blessed Trinity, co-substantial as God with the Father and the Holy Spirit. Therefore, just as a Catholic believes that God exists, that Christ is bodily present in the Blessed Sacrament, that Our Blessed Lady is ever-virgin, *because the Catholic Church teaches this*, so also does he or she believe *with Catholic Faith* 'that artificial means of contraception are always intrinsically evil', because that is the solemn and official teaching of the Catholic Church. If a Catholic ceases to believe what the Catholic Church teaches, when he starts to pick and choose, accepting some teachings and rejecting others, then he loses his Catholic Faith and so ceases to be a Catholic. The classic example of our times is Fr. Hans Kung who, according to official pronouncements of the Holy See, is no longer entitled to call himself a Catholic theologian. (For '*A Common Misconception*', see Appendix A.)

When through holy Baptism a human being becomes a child of God, sharing in God's Divine Nature, i.e. Supernatural Life, then, with this new Eternal Life, the baptised person also receives the *Supernatural Faculties* which enable him or her properly to live that new life for God and with God. Just as we need organs and senses: the brain, the heart, eyes, etc., and natural faculties like intelligence and free will, to live a fully *human* life; so, 'the new creation in God', receives from God, Supernatural Faculties to fully live the new Supernatural Life received from God as a share in His own Divine Nature.

The first and foremost Faculty is the Supernatural, infused, Divine <u>Virtue of Faith</u>, which is a share in the Divine Intelligence, a Supernatural Light; which enables the fortunate recipient to 'see' what God sees and knows, and to believe what God has revealed. *Catholic* Faith, then, is the firm belief, that Christ founded a visible Church on earth and that He vested in the Head of that Church *His own* Divine Authority to authentically *proclaim and interpret* the Sacred Truths He had revealed on earth and had left behind for the salvation of mankind. Thus, for Catholic Faith to exist and flourish, the Magisterium of the Church, that is Her Teaching Authority, is indispensible. So indispensible that Christ guaranteed its *infallibility*.

There is a text in Holy Scripture which gives to this Supernatural Faculty and its acts, Acts of Faith, its overriding importance. "*Faith,*" says the holy author of the Letter to the Hebrews, "*without which it is impossible to please God*". (Hebr. 11:6.)

In the aftermath of the Reformation, faced with the splintering of faith in the Protestant churches after their break-away from the mother Church, *the Council of Trent* was determined to settle beyond doubt the contentious question of 'Faith'. It declared most solemnly with the Authority of Christ Himself:

(1) How to interpret Hebr. 11:6, with these words:

It is our CATHOLIC Faith without which it is impossible to please God". (Denz. Schnm. 1510.)

Before the Reformation, Catholic Faith was synonymous with Christian Faith. Since the Protestant Reformers made a distinction in this, and rejected Catholic Faith, it was up to the Church to authentically declare which faith was the true Christian Faith, coming

down to us from the Apostles. The new 'christian faith' of the Reformers was alien to Christianity prior to the Reformation.

(2) Why Catholic Faith is such a priceless gift from God, with
    these words:

" *…because Faith is the beginning of Salvation of man, the*
foundation and root of all justification, and 'without which it is im-
possible to please God'."

By quoting again the words from Hebr. 11:6, which earlier the
Council had taught must be taken as meaning *Catholic* Faith, the
Council reminds us that She is referring here to *Catholic Faith* as
being the beginning, foundation, and root of all justification. Only
one thing can be the beginning, root and foundation of something
else. By including the word 'all' the Council categorically states
here that Catholic Faith is absolutely necessary not only for the salvation of Catholics, but for everybody's (*ALL*) salvation! The
Council does not say that Protestant faith cannot save. But it does
say that Protestant Faith cannot save *on its own*, but depends on
the existence of Catholic Faith on earth in order to save those who,
by no fault of their own are not baptised into the Catholic Church.
The submission, obedience and humility to the Catholic Church's
teaching shown by *Catholic* Faith are so pleasing to God, that on
the strength of that He will extend the saving grace of Justification
to anyone who sincerely seeks Him and tries to believe in Him with
another faith.

It does not mean that everybody has to be a Catholic in order to be saved. But it DOES mean that everybody who finds himself saved in Heaven, will thank the beginning, root and foundation of his salvation to the Catholic Church and the Catholic Faith within Her. That Faith has its origins at the very beginning of Christianity: *Faith in the Church founded by Christ!* None of the other contenders after the break-away Reformation could qualify for this linear descendancy since no reformer required 'faith' in a church from then on. Consequently no faith was stable for long after that.

This directly means that, if Catholic Faith was to be removed from the earth, no other christian faith, or any other faith, would be pleasing to God; as no other faith is made in submission, obedience and humility to the Catholic Church. If a non-catholic goes to heaven, he will find on arrival before the throne of God, that God justified him NOT on the strength of his own defective faith; but on the strength of the perfect Faith found in our Holy Mother the Catholic Church. This Church alone is the source of all Graces necessary for salvation: everybody's salvation.

Hence the murderous attack on Catholic Faith by MODERNISM.

This solemn teaching of the Catholic Church on Faith in Her, which pertains to Her very foundation, is therefore infallible teaching: teaching infallibly true as having been revealed by Christ. Christ demanded that His authority should be vested in Peter, in the Papacy, *and consequently in the Church headed by Peter, by the Papacy. Christ could never demand Faith in this Authority, if this Authority could fail.* IF THIS CHURCH IS INFALLIBLE IN ITS MOST IMPORTANT TEACHING, THEN THIS CHURCH IS

NEITHER DECEIVED NOR DECEIVER. NEITHER, THEN, IS FAITH IN HER DECEIVED.

Here then emerges the beginning of our answer to the question posed earlier: 'How is it possible that there appear to be so many who, whilst professing to believe in Christ, yet are deceived?'

They can be deceived because they do not believe the way Christ willed them to believe: through Faith in His Catholic Church. Only the Catholic Church demands with the Authority given to Her by Her Founder, that Her believers believe in Her teaching with submission of mind and will, in obedience and humility. Not as a consensus to agree with some majority, but with a consensus to agree with the Teaching Authority itself. Disagree in the Catholic Church with the Magisterium itself, even if you appear to have a noisy majority with you, and you cease to profess your Catholic Faith, the beginning, root and foundation of everybody else's salvation. And if this dissent reaches far enough to include DOGMA: teaching which not only is infallibly true, but has been officially declared to be infallibly true, then you cease to be a Catholic altogether, since you have lost your Catholic Faith …

If the consequences of keeping one's Catholic Faith wholly intact are of staggering importance, so are the consequences of giving it away equally momentous. For both cases are a matter of life and death.

We may now start to appreciate the existence of *global* Evil around us far more bent on the creation of a deceitful *planetary religion*, than on the creation of a one-world dictatorship! The latter creates only misery for this life; the former for Eternity … For this, the matter of 'non-deception' is of ABSOLUTE importance, which was not left by Christ to CHANCE! Non-deception starts with the priceless gift of supernatural, infused, Divine, CATHOLIC Faith, "the beginning, root and foundation of ALL justification, and without which it is impossible to please God". ... But there the matter does not rest.

II

The Catholic Church's Teaching on Philosophy

THE CATHOIC CHURCH appears to be the only Religion which is prepared to give full credit to the human intellect in relation to Supernatural Faith, even allowing for a certain weakening of its penetrating power after the Fall. Human thinking is done according to unbreakable rules willed and established by our Creator, which rules cannot be transgressed without damage to the thinking.

The Catholic Church considers this important, as the human intellect is the seat, the natural *substratum*, for the precious gift of the divinely infused Faith. A PHILOSOPHY studies those Laws and Rules of Thinking, and so it is for the Catholic Church of the utmost importance *which philosophy* is being adopted, since an unsound, defective philosophy will lead to crooked thinking, which in turn prevents the necessary harmony between Faith and its seat; the human intellect.

As we have already seen, the Catholic Church is not deceived in those grave matters pertaining to Faith; that is, pertaining to Catholic Faith in Her. Her views on Philosophy, and so Her teaching on THOMISM, i.e. The Philosophy and Theology of St. Thomas Aquinas, must be considered with the utmost willingness to comply with that teaching. This is not so much because the Catholic Church is concerned with Philosophy as such, but because She is very concerned about the integrity of Catholic Faith; which integrity is impossible to maintain, if that Faith is to be harnessed to the wrong philosophy, to the wrong ideas of reality and to the wrong interpretation of thinking itself. The way the human mind touches on reality is decisive, and our Holy Mother the Catholic Church cannot leave explanations of these matters to chance, doubts and opinions. Consequently, She cannot err in deciding for us which Philosophy contains the Truth about the human mind's acquisition of true knowledge and understanding.

Since nothing on earth can be more important than the *beginning*, the *foundation*, and the *root* of *all* justification; that is, Catholic Faith, the Church's teaching on the preservation and safeguarding of Catholic Faith must be just as absolutely true as Her teaching is about the nature of Faith itself. If, then, for the last 100-odd years the Church has steadfastly taught us that in this area nothing is more important than THE PHILOSOPHY OF ST. THOMAS AQUINAS, we do well, then, to take in this teaching with the utmost seriousness. In my book on *THE FOUNDATIONS OF OUR CATHOLIC FAITH* I have gone through the most important documents of the Church to put before my readers the grave reasons the Catholic Church has brought forward in support of Her teaching on THOMISM.

According to the Church, St. Thomas Aquinas explains to us systematically, and with consistent correctness, how the human mind can know God from His created reality; how that same mind can know itself and is able to discover the rules that govern its thinking activity; how the human mind can correctly understand that man is composed of 'body and soul' and is capable of fathoming the true nature of soul: a created spirit capable of independent existence after death, yet at the same time the life-giving principle of the human body without which it could not come into existence. In other words, the Catholic Church is satisfied that the teachings of St. Thomas on Truth, Morality, Reality, and the whole Unseen World, will lead one to the best preparation for the reception, the acceptance and the preservation of the gratuitous Grace of the Catholic Faith. This preparation, this training in clear thinking, this ground-work and natural anticipation, the Catholic Church calls – with St. Thomas – the *PRAEAMBULA FIDEI*, THE Preambles to the Gift of Faith, the Prelude, or Opening-up to this free Gift from God.

So impressed is our Holy Mother the Church with this complete system of thought, which goes directly to the nature, the essentials and the Truth of things, that She has declared that this Philosophy, as a whole as well as in all its parts:

"seems to chime in, by a pre-established harmony, with Divine Revelation, i.e. With Eternal Truths. No surer way to safeguard the First Principles of Faith." (*Humani Generis*, 1950)

Those words of Pope Pius XII are awe-inspiring.

For one carillon of pealing bells to be in perfect harmony with itself, is already a feast for the ears and an achievement of no mean merit. But here the holy Catholic Church is not talking about a Philosophy: a complete system of Truths, being wholly consistent and in perfect harmony with itself, but of a System of Harmonious Truths being totally consistent and in harmony *with a Divine System of Eternal Truths*! A whole carillon of earthly bells, pealing and chiming in, by a pre-established harmony, with the heavenly carillon of Eternal Truths: Father, Son and Holy Spirit. This is an accolade of such formidable genius that it can only be given to *one* Philosophy, to one philosophical system, as the Crown and glory of all attempts at human greatness: *the Philosophy of St. Thomas Aquinas …*

In the light of this teaching it is not hard to see that the Magisterium of the Catholic Church foresaw, long before the devastations became visible at the lower levels of the rank and file, that 'the enemy of the human race and of human nature' would launch its strongest attack on Catholic Faith *through natural thinking*. Through the wholesale rejection of the pinnacle of that thinking: the Philosophy of St. Thomas Aquinas. For, once the Philosophy "that chimes in with Revelation" was rejected, *nothing*, no other 'philosophy' or thought-system could take its place, since only one philosophy can "chime in with Revelation". Once crooked thinking in defiance of St. Thomas' philosophy would get hold of the human mind, it would be inevitable that the repercussions would be felt in the supernatural level of faith.

This, then, provides us with a further answer to our original question on deception in believers in Christ: *they have not guarded against the wrong philosophy*; against crooked thinking at the lower level; against adopting ways of thinking which militate against Truth, against proper evidence and the laws of reasoning. This way their Supernatural Faith lost its sound substratum; it got undermined, and they started to believe things which are at variance with the Church's teaching. And since 'Catholic Faith', as we saw, is essentially bound up with the Catholic Church, they started to lose their Catholic Faith, whatever gains in other areas they may have thought they would make. Their defective and inadequate HUMAN thinking prevented them from "chiming in with Revelation". And for that reason their Supernatural Thinking, their Catholic Faith, became defective as well.

III

The Catholic Church's Teaching on Our Lady

Here we come across a curious phenomenon. *None of the modernists and teilhardians* at present time in the process of separating themselves from the Catholic Church in order to form their own branch of the one-world 'church of darkness', that 'church' "without dogma, without hierarchy, without discipline of the mind and curb on the passions" (Pope St. Pius X), none of these modernists have any devotion to Our Blessed Lady at all. *They simply can't take Her with them into their new-fangled 'church'!* Is not this the Reformation repeating itself?

On the other hand, by far the great majority of the well-adjusted Catholics, with their steadfast Faith without confusion, their great Hope without dismay, and their unfailing Love even for the destroyers of everything they hold dear; these true and true Catholics, the salt of the earth, all have kept a deep and lasting devotion to the Mother of God. There is no deception possible here:

the true is where Our Blessed Lady is, and only in this one Church is She sure to be surrounded by children wanting to go to Jesus through Her. Over the centuries, as we clearly see repeated today, great devastations in groups and individuals have been brought about by forms of 'renewal' and 'reformation' which rejected, amongst other things, the Church's sure teaching on Our Lady. Such renewals and reformations come from *outside* the Catholic Church as a form of deception from the Devil, "the father of lies". This can clearly be deduced from the fact, that the thought behind such a drive was and still is the conviction, that such a move would do God and Christ a real service in playing down the importance of His Mother. For behind this conviction is the deep-seated deception 'that this would enhance Christ'.

But such thinking and such a conviction not only rejects Our Blessed Lady: even more importantly for the salvation of souls, this thinking *rejects the Catholic Church!* For such a conviction could not be adopted without specifically rejecting clear and unambiguous Catholic teaching from the origins of Christianity. We have already established that the Catholic Church is not deceived in Her teaching, which means that the rejection of the Catholic Church *because of Her teaching*, must reveal a deception in Faith. From (II) above we know that such deception is brought about by erroneous thinking at the natural level: a deception of the human mind.

Let us substantiate this by producing the evidence.

The Tradition of the Church founded by Christ is undeniably MARIAN. And the one who kept that Tradition unbroken is – even today – the Catholic Church. In showing forth its own orthodoxy with regards to the Church's teaching on the Blessed Virgin Mary, VATICAN COUNCIL II went as far back as it is possible to go: to the teachings of ST. IRENAEUS, a disciple of ST. POLY-CARP, who, in turn, listened to the preaching of the Apostle ST. JOHN. According to that teaching, both the Eastern and Western Church believed on Apostolic Authority:

(i)   "that Mary is a cause of our salvation";

(ii)   "that Mary is the New Eve, undoing the 'knot of Eve's sin'";

(iii) "that Mary is a model and proto-type of the Church". (*Lumen Gentium*, ch.8, No. 56, 63.)

Later centuries have undoubtedly enlarged the canvass started by this most ancient teaching of the Church. And with this teaching the devotion of all the ages of Christianity towards the Mother of God was firmly based on the most sound foundation and beginnings. For it was inspired, not so much on Mary's passivity, i.e. On what God had done for His humble Handmaid; but on Mary's active cooperation with Grace, i.e. On what Mary had done for God, and for us, and for our salvation. And no one can quibble with that, for, what Mary had done for God and for us, was *unique* … Space does not permit us to enter here more fully into the incredible riches of this earliest teaching of the Catholic Church on Our Blessed Lady. I have done so in two previous articles: *Our Lady* and *Tradition*, guided by a penetrating study from the hand of a scholar and Priest, Fr. William G. Most: *Vatican II – Marian Council*, St. Paul Publications. But what concerns us most intimately here, I will bring out once again as follows.

We know St. Paul divulged Divine Revelation when, under the direct inspiration from God, he revealed to us the 'New Adam – Old Adam' parallel between Christ and our proto-parent Adam. (Rom.5:12-19.) This revelation includes the exact order-in-reverse of the Redemption as against the Fall, as well as the deep Mystique of the Suffering Servant of Yahweh, expiating the transgressions of many.

We know too that indirectly St. Paul, by revealing this parallel, could not help but point also *to a new Eve*; reversing the role of our proto-mother Eve; for it was impossible not to bring to the minds of the early Christians the roles of the New Eve and the First Eve, when pointing to a Divine Parallel between Christ and the First Adam.

But St. Paul went further and directly drew attention to the intimate relationship between Adam and Eve, *and the difference between them*. With this he gave us a clear indication of the intimate relationship between Christ and His New Eve, and of the difference between the beginning of the Fall and the beginning of the order-in-reverse, the Redemption, *precisely on the question that concerns us uppermost here: THE QUESTION OF DECEPTION …*

In 1 Tim.2:14, St. Paul makes the following very profound observation which has a direct bearing on this question of *deception*, when he wrote:

"Adam was not deceived, *but the woman was deceived*, and that was the way she became a transgressor."

Therefore, one of the very first things the early Christians were bound to associate with the *New Eve*: with the person brought to mind by this text, the woman partaking in the order-in-reverse, Redemption, was *NON-DECEPTION*. And that has stuck!

We already know that St. Paul had an accurate grasp of the opposite ways in which Sin and Salvation came into this world. Here he shows that he is well aware of the difference between the Sin of Eve and Adam's Sin, the latter only becoming *Original Sin*. A sin, not committed under any false illusion. By showing that he knew that the First Woman was deceived by listening to the Fallen Lucifer, St. Paul further reveals that he fully understood that Mary was not deceived by listening to the message of the Archangel that came to Her from God. No pressure was put on Her. Her decision had to be made in complete freedom and in total Faith in God, before God the Son took flesh in Her virginal womb.

After Eve's Sin, Adam's hands were tied: 'the knot of Eve'!

Before Mary's 'Fiat', 'Let it be done', God's Hands were tied, so to speak. He wanted to depend fully on Mary's free consent. And for the second time, for one moment, the fate of the whole human race was in the hands of a Woman: "Would She believe the Angel's story or not?" She believed, and obeyed ... And therein lies all the greatness of Womanhood. The 'knot of Eve' was undone, and the 'hands of God' were untied ...

And when the impact of this Revelation started to become understood by the early Church, there was no longer any holding back: "*THE VIRGIN WAS NOT DECEIVED*" ... And from that moment on, the Catholic Church 'bound herself to the Virgin Mary', so that, in time and eternity, Her children would also never be deceived. And could continue the work started by the New Eve: to undo the 'knot of Eve' in sinners, and to become, like Mary, 'a cause of salvation for the Human Race', in total obedience to Her Head and Her Groom, Jesus Christ. Since Mary is the Mother of the Lamb of God, there is no greater achievement for the Bride of the Lamb of God than to become like Her Mother and Model.

"Not deceived ..."

Now we have the full story. Now we know for sure why Catholics who, on the example of the Early Church, 'bound themselves to the Virgin', are not deceived, but have acquired a powerful relationship with Christ. Far from being alienated from Christ, these Catholics have trusted the teachings of His Church; which include Her teachings on Our Blessed Lady, and have become exactly the Catholics Christ wanted them to be, modelled on the image and likeness of His Mother. For the Lady who was never deceived, and unfailingly followed Her Divine Son all the way to Calvary, can be trusted to do the right thing with His children.

And now we also know why people who run Our Lady down, or who dissociate themselves from a filial devotion to Her, are deceived, even if they imagine they are doing this to please Christ. For they not only reject devotion to Our Blessed Lady: *they reject official and traditional Catholic teaching!* Teaching that goes back, as we saw, to the time of the Apostles, i.e. to the foundations of the Catholic Church. These unfortunate Christians are rejecting Apostolic Tradition in exchange for a 'church' which, to them, may still 'look like the Lamb', but in reality, 'speaks like the Dragon'. A 'church of deception', into which it is impossible to take the Virgin who was never deceived.

Chapter Three

Bound To The Virgin

"*Bound to the Virgin ...*" With these words, taken from the end of the previous chapter, we have laid the foundation for the particular '*Way of Life*', spoken of in the Foreword of this book, and to be studied in its pages: "*The 'True Devotion' of St. Louis Grignion de Montfort*".

We have come a long way for this.

The First Chapter should have convinced us that it is of the utmost importance *not to be deceived.* Not to be drawn by pretexts of 'freedom' and 'human dignity', to the looming one-world 'church of darkness'. Not to forget that '*Planetary Citizenship*' requires a *political religion* which demands apostasy from the Catholic Faith, as *none* of what is best, vital and unique in Catholicism has been taken over by the one-World 'church'.

Ignorance of the Truth is not automatically synonymous with deception. When we are ignorant of the Truth, the magnificent virtue of *Prudence* should stay our hand, and should keep us out of trouble until we have had an opportunity to study and ascertain the Truth. The Modernists who sincerely believe that you can fool all of the people all of the time, will always want you to rush into their latest gimmick with great enthusiasm, since they mistakenly believe that both the rush and the enthusiasm come from the Holy Spirit. (More about this in one of the Appendices at the end of this book.)

The Second Chapter was meant to put before us *how* the Holy Catholic Church wishes us to ascertain the Truth and stay with it.

(i) The first thing to do is to use the magnificent faculty God endowed us with: the human mind, or intellect, and train it according to the tenets contained in the Philosophy of St. Thomas Aquinas. This Philosophy is built on the rules and principles the Creator has built into the human mind to guard it from error. E.g. The human mind will not accept that the two parts of a true contradiction are equally true. The Modernists have introduced into the Catholic Church hordes of propositions which contradict Catholic Teaching, wanting them to be accepted as 'equally true'. Here the human intellect can give invaluable assistance to Catholic Faith. Long before ones Catholic Faith becomes involved in such disputes, the clear-thinking mind should have rejected those preposterous 'doctrines' as unworthy of consideration, since they offend Catholic Truth, and so also the human intellect.

According to the truthful teaching of the Catholic Church, this beautiful Philosophy contains within itself the 'Praeambula Fide', that is; all that, which *opens up* the mind of man to Catholic Faith, prepares the way to it, makes him hungry for it, and will set him on the road in search of it. No wonder, then, that the Enemy of human nature was hell-bent on the destruction of this most powerful aid. For these Preambles of the Faith "chime in, by a pre-established harmony, with Revelation itself. *No surer way* to safe-guard the First Principles of the Faith itself"! (Pope Pius XII.)

(ii)   Once the priceless gift of Catholic Faith has been granted by Almighty God, then nothing of what was said in (i) above will be destroyed or rendered useless; *it is to be maintained at all cost*, to play its indispensable but subor-dinate role to the Supernatural Light of Faith itself. The supernatural way of coming to all the Revealed Truths and to stay with them, is to develop one's Catholic Faith to the full by the usual means: prayer, penance, obedience to the Church's Teaching Authority, the frequent reception of the Sacraments. In practice this means 'staying with the Catholic Church', making full use of all the natural and Supernatural means at one's disposal. And in this age of rampant deceit and paralysing confusion, 'staying close to the Virgin who was never deceived': the Blessed Virgin Mary, Mother and Model of the Church founded by Christ.

Taken together these two means of coming to the Truth –

(i) the clear thinking of the well-trained mind, and

(ii) the super Light of a well-formed Catholic Faith,

- are but two sides of the *one* coin: the invaluable possession of *The Discipline of the Mind*, the absence of which was made by Pope St. Pius X as one of the 4 hallmarks of the one-World 'Church of

Darkness': that 'church' built on deception, the exact and total opposite of the Church, of which the Blessed Virgin Mary is both the Mother and Model.

This combination of the fully developed natural and Supernatural Light in 'the Discipline of the Mind', is the most powerful thing on this earth. It will resist and finally overcome 'the beast that looks like the Lamb but speaks like the Dragon': that false, 'political' religion of 'planetary citizenship', which will do everything in its power to subjugate the human race to Antichrist, Satan's most powerful seed.

It is my intention to view the *'True Devotion'* of St. Louis Grignion de Montfort in the Light of the *'Discipline of the Mind'*. In the light of clear human thinking as well as in the Light of Catholic Faith. In the former I will advance the 'Praeambula': all that, which makes it intellectually satisfying; which makes it *naturally* attractive, and inducive to acceptance. In the latter I will bring out how the Supernatural Light of Catholic Faith will support the earlier findings, and will complete and sublimate this 'way of life' as viewed from Eternity.

And for those who still need an 'Introduction' to this most powerful aid to personal holiness, here are the authentic words of St. Louis de Montfort himself:

Perfect Consecration to Jesus Christ

"As all our perfection consists in being conformed, united, and consecrated to Jesus Christ, the most perfect devotion is, naturally, that which conforms, unites and consecrates us most perfectly to him.

And, as Mary is, among all creatures, the one most conformed to Jesus, it follows that devotion to Her is the one that best consecrates and conforms a soul to Her son. Therefore, *the more a soul is consecrated to Mary, the more it is consecrated to Jesus.*

This is why perfect consecration to Jesus is nothing less than perfect consecration to Mary – which is the devotion I teach and preach – or, let us say, the perfect renewal of the vows and promises of Baptism.

This devotion consists in giving oneself entirely to Our Lady, so that we may belong entirely to Jesus through Her. We must give Her our body, with all its senses and members; our soul, with all its faculties; our goods and riches and all we shall acquire; and all our inner assets, such as merits, virtues and the good works we have done or may do ... We must reserve nothing ..."

I

The Preamble to the True Devotion

Here it is our intention to bring the first part of the Discipline of the Mind to bear on the subject-matter at hand. To gather evidence to convince the human mind that the 'True Devotion' is based on natural truth, which makes it a good, desirable for the human will in its quest for its own ultimate end. If this devotion is such an outstanding spiritual good, as the numerous testimonies of competent Spiritual Directors make us believe it is, then it must be possible for the human mind to collect evidence to that effect, *which will make the acceptance in the Supernatural Light of Faith so much easier.* (The subject-matter of the second part of the 'Discipline of the Mind'.)

Why this process of 'Preambles'? Of finding natural truths and evidence first? Because, if this is not done, and, because of this neglect, a good has been rejected, then there is every chance that a first rate *Supernatural* Good could have been cast away. Imagine a priest refusing to have anything to do with the 6 Apparitions of Our Lady at Fatima, and consequently rejecting their Supernatural value and origin. What a great spiritual good for himself and others is he missing out on. Where a proper investigation would have opened up the mind of that priest to Faith in those Supernatural realities, would have prepared the way for their acceptance in Faith, would have made him hungry for the Supernatural benefits, and would have put him on the road to a proper Supernatural investigation in the Light of Faith, (the second arm of the Discipline of the mind), there is now emptiness in disbelief.

On the other hand, imagine the great *spiritual* harm that would be prevented, if a proper investigation *on the natural level* protected a person from credulity, and from rashly following an unapproved 'apparition' …

Let us then allow the human mind to do its homework first, and let it arrive at a *natural* understanding of the 'True Devotion', which is called the preamble to a proper Supernatural investigation, and consequent acceptance, in the Light of Faith. That was the way St. Thomas allowed the natural Truths of his Philosophy, his 'preamble to the Faith', to "chime in with Revelation".

The late Frank Duff, in a 'Foreword' to a particular edition of St. Louis de Montfort's *True Devotion*, has done precisely what we are about to do ourselves: he has collected evidence, historical and otherwise, which makes the 'True Devotion' humanly credible and acceptable.   And with a truly Thomistic, i.e., properly trained mind, he brings out arguments in favour of the Devotion, and demolishes objections raised against it.

"Because Louis-Marie de Montfort is a latter-time Saint, many think that his system of devotion is a comparatively modern development.   But he disclaims having originated the devotion or any aspect of it.   He gives examples of persons who, 700 years before his own days, had made the Consecration after the same fashion he recommends.   Moreover, he asserts that the idea was not new even then: he quotes Boudon as saying that it went still further back in that precise form.   Finally he claims that the idea would spring naturally from the very foundations of Christianity.   From this it is to be understood that the True Devotion is no new invention of a few centuries ago."

This is the beginning of sound reasoning, and we must leave this particular historical argument rest here, as we have neither the place nor the time to bring out all the evidence St. Louis and Frank Duff had for their assertions.   But we will come back to this matter later on in the second part, when we will follow the reasoning, *aided by the Supernatural Light of Catholic Faith*, how exactly the True Devotion can be traced back to "the very foundations of Christianity", i.e. "how it chimes in with Revelation".   Let us first continue to use our natural intellect to follow another line of argument.

"This makes the True Devotion ancient enough, but possibly not enough to dispel the uneasiness of those who think that it, and Mariology in general, belong to an era of Catholic departure from primitive purity of doctrine. Most of that school assign the 5th or 6th century as the time when Mariology began to appear. When we analyse this accusation closely, it becomes evident that the date-line in their mind is the Council of Ephesus (431 AD), and that they believe that it ushered in a new and incorrect tendency, which proceeded to take destructive possession.

But they are totally misconstruing that event and its surrounding situation. To the extent of *reversing the facts*. It is senseless to suppose that everything new in the way of doctrine began from Ephesus. The Council only put into the form of a definition something which the ordinary Catholic people had in perfect perspective, but which certain innovators were trying to twist out of its original shape. It was the Nestorians who were the disturbers and who were condemned. *It was the old belief which was defined and which continued.* Cardinal Newman gave us a list of Saints from the 1st Century up to Ephesus whose utterances on this subject would be identical with what would be said after Ephesus. St. Augustine, addressing the Virgin, would typify them: '*He who made Thee, is made in Thee*'."

This too is again a purely historical argument which does not involve doctrines of Faith, and can be verified and accepted by anyone who believes in the Truth, even if not endowed with the Supernatural Light of Faith. Frank Duff then continues with a Supposition, for which he brings out some evidence.

"I suppose that it was the conversion of the Empire about 300, which really threw the Church into its problems. The open proclaiming of the Faith brought with it the opportunity of criticising it and to dissent from it. This tendency would be stimulated by the fact that the wind of official favour would waft into Christianity many elements which were not fervent, and perhaps worse than that. So every day brought its new light and its new error, with corresponding need for correction by the Church. But where the other denominations of Christianity *deceive themselves*, is in the supposing that this process of correction and development represented a deviation from earlier perfection."

Frank Duff is on solid ground here. Underlying the perpetual and sometimes vehement struggle is the determination of the ordinary Catholic Christians *to see the Ancient Doctrine kept in all its purity*, uncontaminated by newfangled twists which do not bear the stamp of Tradition. Prepared to do battle to prevent a spurious interpretation to come in and take over the original Faith, they look around for all the weapons common sense, history and Tradition will teach them have been effective in the past. And the weapon *par excellence* for the last 2000 years has been *recourse to the Mother of God, the Virgin who was never deceived*. ... It flies in the face of historical evidence for any Protestant to claim that he or she is the inheritor of Original Truth. On close scrutiny they will find out that they are the keepers *of the pruned-off false growths* ... We will come back to this more deeply (again) when dealing with Doctrine.

Historical arguments, as convincing as they are, are not the only recommendations to a singular devotion to Our Blessed Lady.

We may point to an obvious advantage that it is wise and prudent to stay close to someone who has never been deceived. For, it is written in Holy Scripture:

"If you have found a man of understanding, visit him early, and wear out his doorstep with your frequent visiting", (Eccles.6:36),

then how much more appropriate is that advice with respect to someone 'who was *never* deceived'? If

"Blessed is the man who is mindful of wisdom,
And who sets himself to acquire understanding.
Who pursues her like a scout,
And lies in wait by her paths.
Who looks in on her through her windows,
And listens at her doors.
Who lodges close to her house,
And drives his tent pins in her walls".

If

"Such a man pitches his tent at her side,
And selects her as his neighbour".

If

"Whoever fears the Lord will act like this ..." (Eccles.14:20-15:1),

what, then, must be said about the one who acts like this in respect to the Blessed Virgin Mary, the Seat of Wisdom?

And finally, how appropriate to the subject-matter at hand: the total Consecration to Our Blessed Lady in order to become totally consecrated to Christ Himself, is the ready-made advice in one of the Books of Wisdom:

"But you, my son, put your feet into her (Wisdom's) fetters,
And your neck into her harness.
Put your shoulders under her yoke and carry Her,
And be not irked by her bonds!
Yes, approach her with all your soul,
And keep her ways with all your might.
Go after her and seek her and she will reveal herself to you.
Once you hold her, *do not let her go!*
For in the end you will find rest in her,
And she will be your joy.
Her fetters will be your strong defence,
Her harness a robe of honour.
Her yoke will be a golden ornament,
Her reins, purple ribbons." (Eccles.6:24-31.)

How more totally could one person be tied to another, on Divinely inspired advice? Fetters, harness, yoke, bonds, reins ... If created wisdom has often been identified, even in the earliest Church, with the Blessed Virgin Mary, then this total Consecration to Our Lady has not only lived as an inspiration in the earliest Christian times: it has, as all God's genuine inspirations, its roots *deep in the Sacred Pages of the Old Testament!* This is sound human advice that anyone, who received from God the natural light of an ordinary intellect, can understand. Yet, the mystery is such, that even the greatest Light in Supernatural, Infused, Divine, Catholic Faith cannot fathom the Wisdom God has expressed in these Sacred Quotations. Which only goes to show that *both parts* of the Discipline of the Mind: the natural understanding as well as the Supernatural Insights, are necessary to comprehend the Wisdom of St. Louis de Montfort's Consecration to Our Lady.

We have seen some of the 'natural understanding'. Let us now turn our attention to the contemplation of the 'Supernatural Insights'.

II

What the True Devotion Reveals in the Light of Faith

Encouraged, then, by the discovery that the natural light of human understanding can find no objections to the True Devotion, since it has Wisdom, Prudence and Truth on its side as well as a long history of adherents, we may feel confident that this 'natural understanding' of the True Devotion, this *preamble* to it, will 'chime in with Revelation'. Now, in the Supernatural Light of our God-given Faith, we must further our investigations, and discover how God sees this relationship between a soul and the Mother of His only-begotten Son. Two things stand out:

(i)   The 'natural understanding', however free from error, is in itself not enough, but only serves as a preamble to viewing the important matter at hand 'sub specie Aeternitatis': in the Light of Eternity.

(ii) We are also conscious of the fact that, if the natural light of human intelligence had discovered any *contradiction, falsehood, immorality or any other reprehensible aspect to such a devotion,* a further investigation in the Light of Faith would be totally superfluous and unnecessary, as it would never make up for what God had already rejected as defective at the lower level. God's Truth is but one, and it is the Eternal Crime of the modernists to force Catholics to live with severe contradictions at the level of their Faith, because of the adoption of grave falsehoods at the natural level, due to the teilhardian rejection of sound thomistic philosophy and principles. So great is the support and defence the Philosophy of St. Thomas gives to Catholic Faith, that anything which contradicts its principles and major tenets *will not chime in with Revelation!* This is the unanimous teaching of the Papacy, as is fully developed in my book: *The Foundations of Our Catholic Faith.*

There can be no doubt that in the Supernatural Light of Catholic Faith, the True Devotion of Consecration to the Blessed Virgin Mary shines forth with such a brilliance, that it throws its dazzling light in all directions. Out of this glorious Supernatural Panorama, I have only room here to select two aspects, which are of fundamental importance to the times in which we live and in which we have to work out our salvation.

A. One aspect goes directly to the heart of the modern problem in the Church.

B. The other pertains to the foundations of our Supernatural Life in God.

A. The Heart of the Modern Problem: A Power Struggle

We know for certain, that on the strength of a false 'philosophy', 'theology' and 'catechesis', *a new 'faith'* is being proclaimed, which we have branded as being no longer the Faith handed down to us from the Apostles. But why? What exactly IS going on? We know of many timid and silent bishops, who are now distinctly siding with the Modernists and have become useless in the area of leadership. They have been overtaken by events, bypassed in understanding, and now the fight simply goes on over their heads.

We know of many weak-kneed pastors who have allowed totally unworthy and self-appointed 'experts' to run away with their liturgy and with their God-given authority over matters of education and discipline in their parishes, without a shot being fired. And once again we realise that the fight has to go on in spite of them. And again we ask:

"But what is the coveted prize?"

From the widespread paralysis in Ecclesiastical circles, we know *that a serious doubt has been cast* as to what constitutes the Catholic Church. The coveted prize is the CATHOLIC FAITH in Her. The Bride of the Lamb of God, our Holy Mother the Catholic Church, has a contender next to Her: a Barabbas, a prostitute called the one-world 'church of darkness', clamouring for recognition. And deceit and confusion are weapons in the hands of the plotters inside and outside the Church, to enforce recognition for the harlot. This makes the 'True Devotion' one of the greatest gifts of Almighty God to our times. *For no such doubt* is in the minds and the Faith of the truly devoted to Our Lady. No doubt as to what constitutes genuine Catholic teaching, and genuine interpretations of VATICAN II, is found in those minds. The greatest gift <u>for the Church Herself</u> to be found in the widespread practice of the 'True Devotion' lies precisely in this: that it expands the love of the Children of Mary from the Model and Mother of the Church to the Catholic Church Herself. This line of defence made up of the "slaves of Mary" will never be broken.

They treat with contempt the rosicrucian syncretism and pseudo-scientific clap-trap which is being passed on as the new and exciting 'catholic insights' in philosophy, theology, catechesis and sex, yes, even with Imprimaturs, like the infamous 'MELBOURNE GUIDELINES', (AUSTRALIA) AND 'CHOICES IN SEX', (England). For they view it as a mockery in the sight of the Almighty to call these insights 'catholic' as much as they consider it an insult, to give the name 'church' to *the Great Apostasy*, which gives to these poisonous new insights both genesis and direction.

The practitioners of the True Devotion to Our Lady are with Her engaged in a struggle which has truly spanned the centuries …

(i) When the Romans started the persecution of the young Church, it was not immediately because they hated Christ, Whom they had never seen, but simply because the *'other-worldliness'* of the Christians proved to be incompatible with their own culture. And in that they saw a challenge and a threat …

However, it must be conceded that the true meaning of that gigantic struggle, and possibly even its outcome, did not escape the discernment of highly intelligent men of that time. Men like Petronius, who may have appeared to outwardly give his approval to the Neronian attempts *to force Christianity to accept the Roman culture of the day as the sole form-giver, the matrix, of religion,* nevertheless had no illusions as to the bankruptcy of that matrix, incapable of producing anything more than corruption. And they viewed with interest the new vitality of the Christians.

The Romans lost because they failed in their attempts to identify Christianity with their pagan culture. Their leaders feared to lose *political* control, if they could not maintain a *political*, State religion …

(ii) And when the great religious battles of the 16th and 17th centuries raged relentlessly over Europe, finally resulting in the segregation of the Lutherans and Anglicans from the Catholic Church, the defeated camp lost again, because they too failed to identify Catholicism with the Renaissance culture of their days. 'EARTH' had been rediscovered, with its laws, art and scientific achievements. But this time, so they claimed, by a process of sublimation through the Christian spirit. "We all agree" could have been the thesis of the intelligentsia of the time, "that it was a futile exercise trying to identify crass paganism of Antiquity with the new Christian spirit. But could not at last a 'REBORN ANTIQUITY': RENAISSANCE, baptised so to speak by christianity, be identified with the Church to make a truly christian civilisation?"

"NO", said the Sensus Catholicus from of old.

"YES", said the new Protestant élan of the day.

But before the 'new religion' found itself rejected as the *political religion* of the Princes, ousted from the Mother Church by the irresistible Force of the Holy Spirit, the battle raged for almost a century, spilling the blood and the fortunes of men. For Satan it was a humiliating defeat. But, unlike 'theologians', Satan learns ….

(iii) "and then, taking Him to a very high mountain, he showed Him all the kingdoms of the world and their splendour. 'I will give you all this,' he said, 'if you fall at my feet and worship me'."

This temptation has been put to the Catholics of our days by Satan, the dethroned, self-appointed ruler of the world. This time it is not so much 'the earth', science, discoveries: this time it is much more. It is the Universe.

Today the temptation "to give the world to the Church in exchange for 'another gospel', and to once again identify the Church with the current world culture, *evolution*," is formidable, and has proved to be too strong for millions of 'proud, modern men'. For *evolution*, as we all know, has paved the way to the greatest unification the world has ever known: *a unification under Evil!*

And it is *evolution* which, through TEILHARD DE CHARDIN, was allowed to appear as pointing beyond itself. It is painted as

being alive and vibrant with 'god'. Its soul is 'god'. Evolution,
then, is the unifying force of our culture. Everything has been subjected to it: 'philosophy', morality, science, education, religion, as
well as the thinking of millions of catholics. Everything ... Except
one thing: the Catholic Church.

And the burning question put before the pagans of ancient
Rome, put before the world of the Renaissance, is now once again
and for the third time placed before the world, the world of our
days:

"Is now at last 'Creation', the Universe, suitably dressed up to
be identified with the Catholic Church? Have we now found, at
last, the true meaning of the Catholic Church, as it was in the Mind
of Christ? A church growing towards identification with the world,
and with every religion within it, to complete Evolution?"

"To say 'NO' now, in the face of this splendour and technologi-
cal magnificence is simply absurd!" is the ruling mentality of the
intelligentsia of today. Evolution, teilhardian evolution that is,
baptised by this unparalleled 'catholic' genius, this second 'Thomas
Aquinas', has proved conclusively (!) that this whole Creation is
more than just 'creation': it is alive with 'god'! At last, OUR culture
appears to be more than just 'culture': *it is the very matrix in which
the identity between Church and Creation is born and formed.* Everything is the 'Divine Milieu'.

This time the temptation to agree is formidable. This time the
very credibility of the Magisterium is at stake ... Shall the Church
say "NO"?

And the 'theologians' have decided: "This time it is too important. This time the Church simply cannot say 'NO'. *This time*

we will not let Her say 'NO'. We will answer the question for Her. And then whoever says 'NO' after our clear 'YES', in contradiction to us, is obviously out of his mind and a nuisance to world unity: Anathema Sit! Away with him, crucify him!"

And in the turmoil, the shouting and the confusion in the 'church of darkness', the clear 'NO' of the Catholic Church got lost. She will not bow down to adore Satan in return for a world he no longer owns. If Christ paid a high price for its Redemption, the Church is equally prepared to pay the same price for its deliverance.

And when, on the invitation of the teilhardian, apostate 'theologians', speaking now world-wide for the Church, the prince of this world will take up his place in the newly formed 'church of darkness', he will find the world unified in political, economic and religious slavery, and he will finish the job of unification by persecuting those who refused to bow their knee and their minds before him. The 'hour of the Church' will be terrible when it finally comes, but She will be under the steadfast protection of the Virgin who was Herself never deceived, and who did not allow Her faithful servants to succumb to deception either.

The Virgin is not only the Mother of the Bride of the Lamb of God, but also Her model and Proto-type. This contrasts irrevocably with the nature and the most secret purpose of the 'church of darkness': *to be the harlot of the Beast!* Preferred by 'modern man', that pathetic end-product of a faked evolution, in preference to the Catholic Church. And the fury of the harlot and the beast will be such, that DANIEL could predict in the Holy Spirit "that the Perpetual Sacrifice will be abolished for three-and-a-half years", the exact time-span allotted by St. John in the Book of Revelations to the reign of the beast.

All this then goes to show, that a power struggle is going on between the deceivers of the First Chapter and the Servants of Our Blessed Lady, who are protected against deception because of their filial love for the Catholic Church. The deceivers may claim to believe in Christ, but they will never project themselves as servants of Our Lady, and so they invariably will end up adoring the fictitious 'cosmic-christ' of Teilhard in their very own 'church of darkness'.

This power struggle is not only over the 'mind of man', but even more importantly over 'who will possess the Catholic Church'. The teilhardian modernists and marxists? Trying to convince the world that they have 'the numbers'? And that the Catholic Church has become the prize possession of their 'church of darkness'? Or the true children of the Church, the Children of Mary? The ones who may be depicted as being the losers, as having been abandoned by their own Church, when a great number of their fellow catholics also "will run after the Beast" (Rev.13:3), and follow it into the 'church of the Second Beast, for the adoration of the First Beast: Antichrist'.

In that fatal hour, how many will bless the great Mother of God for the singular grace of having made their total consecration to Her in plenty of time, which will enable them to unfailingly know where the Catholic Church is to be found at any given time, no matter how great the confusion or how deep the darkness all around them.

For the True Church will always look like Our Lady, will always be modelled on Her, will always be protected by Her, and will always be illumined by the Supernatural Light of Catholic Faith.

B. Union With God

For a Catholic there is no other road to God, and to union with God, than through the Catholic Church. Try as we may to make up our own minds in these things: unless we Catholics believe in the teachings of the Catholic Church, and unless we order our lives according to that teaching, we will find no other way to Christ, and through Christ to God. If the True Devotion makes a Catholic wide-eyed to see where, at any time, the Catholic Church is to be found, and makes him willing to comply with all Her teachings, then the True Devotion, far from detracting from Christ, is for Catholics a powerful means, willed by God, *to remain with His Son in the Church founded by Him.*

But there is even more to it than this.

The greatest Union with God is in Holy Communion, and Marian Catholics are invariably Eucharistic Catholics. Nearly all of them are daily communicants, brought to the Table of the Lord by their love for the very one who gave us Christ in the Incarnation. Here there is no deception possible: the True Devotion does not stop at Mary, but leads one directly to God. Therein lies the great secret: that the True Devotion *is willed by God* for the glorification of His Mother. It is as safe for the salvation of souls as staying in the Catholic Church. For that is its final end.

Our Blessed Lady is, in God's saving Will, not only the Mother of the Sacred Humanity of His only-begotten Son Jesus Christ; but is, at the same time, also the Mother of His Mystical Body, the Catholic Church. Christ is the Head of His Church; and no one is only the mother of the head of a body. Abandoning Our Lady 'for the sake of ecumenism' is the beginning of one's departure from the Catholic Church, *AND FROM THE TRUE ECUMENISM WITHIN HER*, for the sake of the false one. And we know in which 'church' the false ecumenism will be found!

Turning to Our Lady is turning to the origin of our Union with God. For it was through Her that God came to us in Christ His Son. Since it is Christ's will that we have union with the Father through Him, it is His ardent desire that we come to Him through His Mother, as He came to us through Her.

There is a great mystique behind this True Devotion. Christ wishes us to come to Him *through His Church*. That is why it is 'His ardent wish' that we have a great devotion to His Mother, *as we can always recognise the True Church in Her* … She is the Mother of the Church founded by Him, modelled on Her. And VATICAN II has taught us once again from the origins of Mariology:

"This Maternity will last *without interruption* until the eternal fulfilment of all the Elect …" (Lumen Gentium. 62.)

WITHOUT INTERRUPTION … No 'moratorium', then, for the sake of ecumenism. No watering down, 'playing it cool', discrete silences, public embarrassments and even downright resentment, yes, even hostility, where devotion to Our Blessed Lady is concerned. These are neither the teachings of the Church, nor the wish of the faithful, nor the will of God. Where these things are found, the 'Sensus Catholicus', the Catholic Instinct, is fast waning, followed by loss of Catholic Faith altogether.

If then there is no obstacle, no impediment, no *interruption* even in the Mind of God to the True Devotion, people are allowed to be in love with the Virgin, who is their Mother, in a most intimate way:

"For She is a breath of the Majesty of God,
Pure emanation of the Glory of the Almighty,
Hence nothing impure can touch Her.
She is the reflection of the Eternal light,
Untarnished mirror of God's active power,
The image of His perfection.
Although alone, She can do all.
Herself unchanging, She makes all things new.
In each generation She enters into holy souls,
Forming them into friends of God, and prophets.
For God loves only those who live with Wisdom.
She indeed is more splendid than the sun;
She outshines all the constellations
Compared with light, She takes precedence,
For light must yield to night,
But over Wisdom evil will never triumph!
She deploys Her strength from one end of the earth to the other.
It is She who orders all things for good.
She it was I loved and searched for from my youth.

I resolved to have Her as my bride,
For I fell in love with Her beauty.
She glories in Her noble birth,
For She lives in communion with God,
And the Lord of all has loved Her.
Yes, she is an initiate in the mysteries of God's knowledge,
Making choice of the works He is to do ..." (Wisdom.7:25-
8:4.)

We know that, if these inspired prayers for Wisdom in the Ancient Regime, were in God's Providence meant to be prayers for the
coming of the Redeemer, then by the same Providence of God they
were written in such a way, that they became the equally ardent
prayers for the coming of Her who was to be His Mother.

How exquisite these prayers are to honour the Mother of God.
How they refer to the fact that She would never be deceived. How
they extol already in the foreknowledge of God, Her Immaculate
Conception. How they praise Her for being wise in understanding
God's saving will, and to act accordingly.

And so we are allowed to pray to Her, and call on Her, *and
bind ourselves to Her* with these selfsame prayers inspired by God
Himself. For we know these prayers have been answered! Who in
the Old Testament but God, the Author of these Sacred Pages,
could have foreseen that *"making choice of the works He is to do"* ...
would one day be literally true, when God, the Creator of Heaven
and Earth, was Her Child in Nazareth. When every choice She
made, and every work He did in obedience to Her, was most pleasing to the Father. And now the same with us when, through the

True Devotion, we have bound ourselves to Her, and to the Church of which She is the Mother and the Model, and through that Church to God.

Pray for me.

Appendix A

About the Erroneous Opinions of the Modernists with Regard to Infallible Teaching

Every Catholic has known for almost 2000 years that Christ founded His Church to guard against error - against individual and collective error. That is a Dogma of the Church, Revealed Truth. Yet, in every gathering led by the Modernists, the attending catholics are being taught *how to safeguard themselves against alleged errors in the teachings of the Church*: the exact opposite. By some curious new 'principle': the 'Principle of Sameness', the contrary to a Revealed Truth is being held up in those meetings of the 'Synagogue of Satan' as being at least equally true, and thus worthy of consideration; but infinitely more preferable than 'the old Church's teaching', which is then subsequently discarded.

Where does this 'principle' come from, and who introduced it into the mainstream of 'catholic' thinking?

Fortunately for us Professor Dietrich Von Hilderbrand drew the attention of the world's philosophers to a curious phenomenon he had discovered in the writings of the late Teilhard de Chardin. The Professor's observation is contained in his famous Appendix to his book: *Trojan Horse in the City of God*.

"I do not know of any thinker who so artfully jumps from one position to another contrary one, without being disturbed by the jump or even noticing it…"

The Professor did not pursue the matter further, but on closer examination it comes to light, that Teilhard can take up these contrary positions as being equally 'true' because of the totally false meaning he tries to give to the thomistic 'Principle of Identity'; making it into a 'Principle of Sameness'. The thomistic 'Principle of Identity' has as counter-balance for its true meaning the 'Principle of Contradiction'; safeguarding it from the misuse Teilhard tries to give it. The 'principle of sameness' is absurd, illogical, non-existing; but **vital to the Modernists!**

Teilhard's understandable hatred for Thomism is only surpassed by his modernist followers, but at a price: their totally contrary 'system' *will not 'chime in with Revelation'*. No catholic philosophy, theology, catechesis, and no Catholic Faith can be built on it, or maintained by it. Yet, it is everywhere passed on as the 'new, exciting, catholic insights'.

Briefly, then, why introduce such a spurious 'principle' and maintain it at all cost?

The answer is: 'evolution'. Specifically, *Teilhardian evolution.* Teilhard wanted his evolution to give a totally new slant on Catholicism. He literally wanted evolution to take care of everything. Even Christ was subjected to it. (*Le Christique*, 1955, one month before his sudden death in a New York hotel room.) To him, evolution ends up *inevitably* in omega point. We can compare it to a jolly cruise ship: it ends up inevitably in port, no matter what people on board think or do. In evolution *it is all the same* if you believe in two opposites as being equally true. It does not really matter what you believe: evolution ends up inevitably in the same bucket ...

If one listens carefully to the sermons of priests 'tainted with modernism', then this is precisely what we hear. God is being depicted as some kind of weak do-gooder with no rights, only duties to the modernists, and 'understanding' of their position. The 'old Church' had it all wrong. We live in a sinless world from which we have nothing to fear, and when we leave this place after a life of 'social graces', we go straight to heaven .... Does any of this 'chime in with Revelation'?

Jacques Mitterand was right when, in 1969, he told his brother-freemasons that the 'crime' of Teilhard was to have placed man on the altar for adoration ... Only, he approved of it. For in name of this 'crime' the most shocking heresies and immorality are tolerated and even condoned, paving the way for the one-world 'religion' of the Second Beast.

Yet Catholics refuse to see all this as a break with Catholic Tradition and thus as a formal break with the Catholic Church. "contrary 'truths' cannot exist", they have been told by a Pope, the late Pope John XIII, upholding the logic of all ages. Teilhardian evolution does not exist, and so the ascertainment of Truth remains of paramount importance; a matter of Eternal Life or Eternal Death.

Let us now briefly examine how the teilhardian modernists go about holding up the contrary to a Catholic Truth as if it has a superior value; after which the victims of the deceit are 'free' to reject authentic Catholic teaching, and embrace the error as the 'new catholic insight' ...

I have before me one of those handouts, titled: 'CATHOLIC THEOLOGICAL COLLEGE' MP2 Fundamental Moral 11, distributed in one of those horror-seminars to catechists for the abortion of their Catholic Faith. The notes are a resume of the teachings of a book by a non-catholic, titled: *The Authority of the Church and the Freedom of the Conscience of the Faithful,* 1966. In these notes Catholics are being taught how to place themselves above the Pope and the Church is deciding for themselves what they consider 'errors' in the Church's teaching, in order to accept or reject teaching at will: *the exact opposite again of Christ's Immutable Will.* But in doing this these people are identifying themselves with error: the very thing Christ wished His Church to protect the faithful from. And since error is being taught at those seminars *in the name of the Church,* these people are clearly apostates; part of the *great Movement of Apostasy* that Pope St. Pius X saw already fully operational *in every country* of his own time. (*Our Apostolic Mandate,* 1910.) They are the 'Fifth Column', infiltrators in the City of God.

In the notes at hand, the fraud starts off with the following statement, and I quote:

"When the Church does not teach us infallibly, she teaches us fallibly, and fallible teaching is, and has been, open to error."

And then, by way of 'explanation' (!), it is put forward that on the average the Church teaches us infallibly only a few times a century; and that all the rest of the time she teaches us fallibly, which means that we must use our own private judgement to sort out this teaching, and to decide – with our infallible mind??? – what is in error, and so to be rejected. (In other words: Christ could have saved Himself the trouble of founding a Church.)

There are two despicable deceits in this caricature of the Catholic Church. (Remember the odd-looking 'church' that is being built?)

1. One deception lies of course in the sure knowledge of these 'experts', that virtually nobody knows that it is a foundation principle in Logic that no valid conclusions can be drawn from negative premises. (The ruin left over after the destruction of Thomistic Philosophy is universal!)

Premise: When the Church does NOT teach us infallibly.

Let us analyse what is being done here by way of an example. What conclusion is there to be drawn from a statement like this:

"When he is off the drink, he is quite a nice man?"

Meaning: "When he does NOT drink …"

The REAL conclusion is not the lame follow up: 'He is quite a nice man'. The REAL conclusion is the *mental image* we are asked to form of the man: 'When he does NOT drink …'. Are we to conclude that he is usually drunk? Is he trying to kick the habit? Was the last time he had a drink two years ago? Yesterday? NEVER? Do not exclude even the last mentioned possibility, for the above statement could be made if he never had a drop in his life. … As can be gathered, it is impossible to draw any valid conclusion from such a statement; and if it is done, it is a fallacy. Some vindictive, spiteful person, making this statement, could quite well have the intention of implying that the man is usually drunk, wanting us to draw THAT conclusion in order to have an unfavourable impression of him. But THAT CONCLUSION may not be true at all, even if the speaker may have made a true statement. We have no way of CONCLUDING if the man never has a drink, or is usually drunk, or is trying to kick the habit.

Let us now go back to the statement about the Church:

"When the Church does NOT teach us infallibly …"

We have no way of knowing if the Church EVER did not teach us infallibly, or is in the habit of not teaching us infallibly, or is trying to kick that bad habit as Modernism is progressing, or what. Vindictive apostates obviously want us to conclude 'that the Church teaches us infallibly ONLY a few times a century …'; but that conclusion, induced with malice, is just as fallacious as any other conclusion we may care to make. What conclusion is there to be drawn from the statement: "When I do not go fishing …" That I like fishing? Am in the habit of going fishing? May occasionally go fishing? Or never go fishing? Impossible to say. What conclusion can be drawn from a 'contingent fact' that did not happen?

2. The second fraud slipped into these notes and used by these 'experts' is far worse, but VITAL to their argument. They deliberately confuse 'infallible teaching' with 'DECLARED' infallible teaching! This comes to light in what they offer 'by way of explanation'!)

To understand what they are really saying, and what sort of 'logic' they are using, here is an example:

If you get a parcel in the mail which contains a book, and NOBODY around you tells you ('declares') that there is a book in it, then, according to the above 'logic' the conclusion is valid: that there is no book in the parcel.

This, of course, is utter rubbish. If you get Catholic Teaching from the Holy Father, and the Pope does NOT declare that it is infallible teaching, then, according to the above 'logic', the conclusion is valid *'that it is fallible (i.e. not infallible) teaching ...'*

First of all, they once again draw a conclusion from a NEGATIVE premise: NOBODY around you tells you ... The Holy Father does NOT declare ... But then they confuse infallible teaching with 'declared' infallible teaching. Teaching can quite well BE infallible, without ever having been DECLARED infallible. The classic example is our belief in the Perpetual Virginity of Our Blessed Lady. This is so universally understood to be infallibly true by the whole Church, except the Modernists, that the Catholic Church has never bothered to make this into a Dogma of the Faith, by DECLARING it to be infallibly true. However, every time the Holy Father uses this teaching in some Encyclical, or speech, he is using INFALLIBLE teaching, and so is teaching us infallibly. The same goes for countless other teachings.

So now we know what 'conclusion' they wanted us to draw when they started off by stating; "When the Church does NOT teach us infallibly..." No conclusion is valid, but their vindictiveness and spite forces the conclusion on the minds of their hapless victims: 'NEARLY ALL Church teaching is fallible'.

And on this sort of fraud, lies, deception, cunning and absurd logic, seminarians, catechists and the faithful at large are being instructed how to be on their guard against an Infallible Church; Divinely instituted to protect us against such teachers and such errors ...

What 'church' other than a 'church of darkness' can be built on such designs? The thrust of these demons is against *HUMANAE VITAE*, declaring it 'fallible teaching' because, to them, the Holy

Father did not 'declare' it to be infallible. Apart from the fact that the Holy Father did indicate that it really is infallible teaching by demanding "*internal assent from Bishops*" (!), their reasoning and conclusions are preposterous.

But, alas, the one-world 'church of darkness', the 'church' of the Second Beast, demands, as we saw in the First Chapter, one-world immorality: everybody on the Pill under the pretext of 'freedom of conscience …'

Thank God for Divine Providence, having foretold us with His Authority already in 1910: 'that the looming one-world 'church' would use freedom as a pretext to do evil'. (*Our Apostolic Mandate*, Pope St. Pius X.)

Appendix B

"Eli, Eli, Lama Sabachthani?"
Ps 22:1   Mt 27:46

When on the Cross Christ cried out these words in Hebrew, He did not mean to tell the people 'that God had deserted Him'. If he wanted to convey that message, He would have spoken in Aramaic. As it was, many bystanders, not comprehending what He said, thought He was calling on Elias.

It is not unreasonable to assume that the marked conversion of Jewish priests in the very Early Church is due to Christ – always the Teacher – intoning this Psalm for them on the Cross. For they knew Hebrew, and understood what He said. And meant! For once intoned, the minds of His tormentors went with Him through the whole of Psalm 22: *the most graphic description* of the Passion and Death of 'the Servant of God' the Old Testament has left us. And with the super-abundance of Redemption, flowing freely from the Cross with His Blood, the grace of conversion was extended to them.

However, the actual words of the Psalmist do speak of a seeming 'desertion by God'; and I will use them in this Appendix in defence against charges made against orthodox Catholics, accusing them of holding '*that God has deserted His Church*', when they point to alarming and wide-spread devastations caused by the Modernists.

The accusation can come from all sides: from well-meaning but shallow faithful who think the defenders of the Faith are exaggerating; from fellow-travellers of the Modernists who are ashamed of their own lack of fervour and courage, but who are in need of some good-sounding excuse; and with great malice from the Modernists themselves who are determined to put strong opposition off-side with the bishops, and with everybody else, by any means.

To be viewed by many as someone 'who does not trust in the Holy Spirit' hurts, and, what is more, could have some effect in stifling at least some *vocal* opposition to the work of destruction that is going on. As long as the accused, sensitive to this sort of criticism, does not give up *praying* all is not lost. The prayers will at least come to the aid of those who see through the fallacy of the accusation and turn it to their advantage.

The thing to do, of course, is to point out to the accusers that none of the Catholics fighting heresy and immorality today, *have yet gone as far as the Holy Spirit and Christ Himself* in describing the extent of the devastations caused.

The Holy Spirit let St. John predict in the Book of Revelation that there will come a time in which *the whole world* will run after the Beast.

Christ Himself has predicted that there would come a time so evil, that 'the love of many would cool off', and that, if it were possible 'even *His Elect would be deceived ...*'

Add to that what Our Lady said at Fatima about a world-wide spread of error, and what two Popes have said about 'a great movement of apostasy in every country on earth', and 'the smoke of Satan seeping into the Church through the cracks', and I am sure that you can convince any modernist that *no ordinary mortal* would have dared to take it upon himself to describe the alarming situation in such words … So, after all, who may claim to have the Holy Spirit, Christ, the Blessed Virgin Mary and Popes on their side, now that the extent of the ravages has been *infallibly* declared *to be world-wide* with God's Authority?

But yet, heresy IS being taught in almost every classroom, from almost every pulpit, in almost every country … Many of the listeners are innocent children, ordinary, simple Catholics; who are not up to the subtleties they hear from all sides. May we not turn the charge from an, admittedly, unwarranted accusation, then at least to a serious problem many people will have in their own private lives? How does one square-off the global lapse into religious anarchy with the Love and Providence of God?

The difficulty is not new. Many a Protestant now would have been a Catholic if his fore-father had remained true to the Catholic Faith. But someone slipped up, did not do his God-given duty; *and for 400 years* his off-spring did not receive the grace of Catholic Faith, *innocent as they were to the effects of this ONE sin of apostasy!* From this we may gauge how seriously God views the priceless gift of Catholic Faith. *Every grace* is given to a Catholic to maintain it and use it for the purpose for which it was granted. If the consequences of keeping it are of such eternal importance, so are the consequences of losing this most precious Gift from God!

Herein lies, of course, the beginning of an answer. God does not abandon His Church. His Church will never abandon Him, no matter how many millions of Catholics may desert Her. Each of these Catholics will recognise in Eternity, that they had at their disposal all the Graces necessary to remain faithful to their Faith.

When the Church shrinks in numbers, the quality of the Faith remaining in Her increases daily, to make up for the loss; so that no one can accuse God of not having looked after him when the Catholics, to whom his Eternal Fate was entrusted, fell by the way-side. There will always be a Catholic Church, with strong Catholic Faith within Her, to cater for everybody, even the heretics!

Finally, No One will be in Hell by accident, because of someone else. And herein lies the complete answer to our problem. We recognise what is being done to children all over the world, to the simple Catholics … Let us look at an answer given by one who is a recognised leader in his field:

"Lore Noto: actor, producer, well-recognised figure in the theatre world, and severe critic of what is taking place on the stages and screen of the entertainment media …

Lore Noto blows away like bubbles from a child's ring every argument that a deprived childhood makes for a troubled adult. Raised from an early age in the Brooklyn Home for Children, and forced, upon leaving, to work in his father's poolroom, he has become a man of stature, with deep moral convictions. He is also a father and feels an obligation to the youth of this country, to speak out on the turn that the entertainment business has taken …

"'Through the world of entertainment' Noto said, 'today's youth are being hammered at, they are being subverted, they are being exploited, they are being manipulated. *But there is ultimately within every human being that need to stop and assess and evaluate and criticise and judge. And that will be the only hope. What does that mean to parents? We have to continually remind them that that is what their responsibility is'."* (*The Embattled Parent*, Gloria Lenz, pp.15,18.)

Recognise it?

For well over 100 years, as we have seen, the Popes have been telling us that the destruction of Supernatural Faith would come through a devastating attack on *clear thinking*, and on the pinnacle of that clear thinking: *the Philosophy of St. Thomas Aquinas.* And we have been told why that Philosophy is so important. Because it is the *preamble* to Faith, the opening up to it, the sound preparation to it; containing Truths with which Eternal Truths *will chime in!* And here is an ordinary man with a penetrating mind, and a love for children, telling us exactly the same. "but there is ultimately <u>in every human being</u> that need to stop, and let clear thinking take over …" And God's Grace, earned by the Church who kept that Philosophy, and the Faith built on it, will then do the rest; and allow these feeble beginnings of clear thinking 'to chime in with His Eternal, Saving, Life-giving Truths, necessary for Salvation'. And accept the surrender to it …

And confining ourselves to 'the Catholic children in the classroom', and to 'the simple-minded Catholics in the pews', hearing all those subtleties, then we must say; that Catholic Faith cannot be taken away from them against their will, but can only be surrendered voluntarily. Somehow, sooner or later, they will be placed before a clear choice; which will put them on either the road to ruin or the road to riches. And long before Catholic Faith will be involved, that choice will be something that pertains to clear thinking. Ultimately, when all is said and done, the road to ruin is taken *because of a want to take it* Prayers are being neglected, temptations, occasions of sin, are not resisted or avoided because of a hankering after these things. The Faith is not studied because of a desire to rather remain ignorant. Clear thinking is blurred, and the Faith suffers. But even here, as Noto says, there can still come a time that the need for reconsideration is strongly felt.

May someone else's heroic virtue then win the day.

Appendix C

Venerable Anna Catharina Emmerich

Obedience to Church authority and Prudence are essential in dealing with all 'private revelations'. In these times of rampant confusion and deception, there is an understandable tendency to cling to these things for 'insight' and 'comfort'.

In the case of the visions and pronouncements of the Ven. A. C. Emmerich, who lived from 1774 – 1824 mostly in Dulmen, Germany; God in His Providence, has taken certain precautions Himself, which must be taken into account for a complete assessment of this particular case of 'private revelation'.

For one, nobody can, strictly speaking, quote the Servant of God directly, since she never wrote down a single thing. In her case, therefore, everything depends on the competence and the authority of the author who wrote about her, and from whose book the quotes are taken.

The *competence* of Father Carl E. Schmoeger, CSsR, her foremost biographer, is as good and trustworthy as any other trustworthy, competent author.

The *authority* of this Priest is enhanced by the favourable circumstances surrounding his work. As I have already made known in the appropriate place in this book, the French translation was made by the Vicar General and Canon of the Cathedral of Versailles from the original German text; and His Holiness Pope Pius

IX *ordered* the Italian translation to be made from the German proof sheets.

Add to this,

- That a poetical genius, Clement Brentano was moved by God to devote his great talents to the service of this Servant of God for years, even long after her holy death,
- That this holy nun was subjected to two very thorough and painful examinations during her lifetime, the results of which were made available to Fr. Schmoeger on the express wish of the then Bishop of Limbourg,
- That the cause for her beatification was accepted by His Holiness Pope Leo XIII,
- And that she was beatified by Pope John Paul II on 3 October, 2004. (Ed. Postscript added to the original text of this book that was printed in 1982.)

And we have all the necessary ingredients on which obedience and prudence depend.

To sum up, then, in making use of the life story of this holy nun, I am not quoting her directly, but I am making quotes from a book which has all the necessary qualifications of authority, competence, historical veracity and accuracy that are needed to guarantee its authenticity.

Appendix D

On Garabandal

I include a brief discussion of this topical matter in these pages because devotion to Our Blessed Lady and deception do not go together. If Our Lady did not appear in Garabandal, then all those promoters of the cult are deceived. Yet how can they claim to have such great devotion to Our Lady, and even seem to display it? What is the situation here?

The situation is that, on the principles of *obedience* and *prudence*, established in the previous Appendix, both the cult and the promotion of Garabandal must be rejected.

There is overwhelming written evidence available that the competent Church authority has steadfastly declared that the events at Garabandal have no Supernatural origin and has steadfastly refused to reconsider its verdict. Also in the most recent letters to come from the office of the Bishop of Santander, dated May 23, 1980, it is categorically stated that the present Bishop

- agrees with the previous Bishops;
- does not approve of the groups in favour of Garabandal;
- has not given anyone permission to spread the cult;
- declares that no further investigation has taken place in the last 4 years.

Furthermore, the letter from Card. Franjo Seper, Prefect of the Congregation for the Sacred Doctrine of the Faith to Archbishop Philip M. Hannan of New Orleans, Louisiana, dated April 12, 1970, is also widely known.

In this letter Card. Seper declares that the Holy See:

- has carefully studied the proceedings of the Bishop of Santander;
- agrees with the definitive negative findings of the Curia of Santander;
- has praise for the prudence shown and the methods followed by the Bishop;
- has no intention of taking over the investigation, or examining this question any further, as the local Ordinary has complete jurisdiction and so the final responsibility;
- has not appointed an 'Official Private Investigator of Garabandal';
- has never approved, even indirectly, the Garabandal movement; has never blessed or encouraged Garabandal promoters or centres; but
- rather deplores the fact that certain persons and institutions persist in fomenting the movement *in obvious contradiction* with the dispositions of ecclesiastical authority, and thus disseminate *confusion* among the people, especially among the simple.

In the full light of the above it can now be categorically stated that any 'fomenters of the Garabandal promotion movement' have no real love for Our Blessed Lady, and so are not examples of people who are deceived whilst having a great devotion to the Mother of God. Rather they are deceived because of their lack of obedience and prudence, and their lack of genuine love and devotion. How can we be so sure?

Because Garabandal directly opposes Fatima, and, being built on sin and deception, was created for the very purpose of discrediting Fatima. The promoters only promote themselves, and their own ego and importance.

How does Garabandal directly oppose Fatima?

When Our Lady first appeared at the Cova da Iria, on the 13th of May, 1917, She said i.a. that she would make known in October who She was, and what Her requests are.

HER VERY FIRST REQUEST made known to the world in Her October apparition was for mankind TO STOP SINNING! Anyone who refuses to stop committing sins, has nothing to do with Fatima; and more precisely, with Our Lady of Fatima. Deliberate *disobedience*, and the deliberate dissemination of *confusion*, (words used by Card. SEPER, the highest authority under the Pope in these matters), are serious sins; and so preclude anyone who commits them from having a genuine love for Our Lady, because such people do not even heed Her most serious request, the one first mentioned at Fatima.

Every time Father Benac, a priest specifically mentioned in a letter from the Bishop of Santander as not having received any permission to promote Garabandal, holds up a stone for kissing 'as having been touched and blessed by Our Lady at Garabandal', he commits a grievous sin of deception. Our Lady never appeared at Garabandal, nor did She touch or bless any stones there …

A few comments for added interest.

1. I know of one person who will testify to the fact that he and his mother lost all love for Our Lady of Fatima as soon as they started to promote 'the apparitions of Garabandal'. The change was so marked, that it pulled him up just in time, and on sorting things out with his mother, they decided not only to stop their Garabandal activities, but also to take steps to undo what damage they may have done in the few weeks they spent recommending the false 'apparitions' to others.

2. Some people are puzzled by the fact, that Rome does not take an independent hand in sorting out alleged apparitions. It worries them that Roman authorities seem to leave it all up to the local bishop, and then accept his verdict as final. Everybody knows that the Garabandalists are constantly promising a 'fresh Roman investigation' which will overturn the findings of the local Ordinary. But not only is nothing forthcoming in this area: Card. Seper has categorically declared that nothing of the sort would be forthcoming. Is there any reassurance to be gained in this situation?

Card. Seper has expressed the correct attitude of the Church in these matters, in line with procedures always adopted. We do not have only Card. Seper's word for that: I know of two instances, where we have Papal testimony to reassure us, that the line adopted in the Garabandal investigation is the official one. Rome will always remain fully informed by the local bishop about the way he went about following official guidelines, set out by the Holy See to be adopted in cases like that. That way, Rome can point out to the local Ordinary in which way his 'homework' could be improved, if necessary.

Here, then, are the two instances, referred to above.

(i) On the occasion of the centenary of the Apparitions of Our Blessed Lady at Lourdes, Pope Pius XII issued a Jubilee Encyclical on 2nd July, 1957. In recalling the history of those blessed events one hundred years earlier, the Holy Father had this to say:

"You know too how firm and pure was the testimony she (Bernadette) bore and how, after being prudently tested *by the episcopal authority*, it was sanctioned *by that authority* as early as 1862. ..."

No mention of Rome sanctioning anything. From start to finish, it was left under the Jurisdiction of the local Ordinary. Rome accepted the final verdict, and, together with the whole Church, rejoiced.

(ii) The same Holy Father is instrumental in producing another proof to the same effect, this time of *his own compliance* with procedures laid down by the Church for the guidance of us all.

In 1942, the Bishop of Namur, Belgium, had completed his investigations into the alleged apparitions of Our

Blessed Lady at Beauraing, and found them worthy of cre-
dence. It was his intention, however, to make his approba-
tion of the heavenly visitations by the Virgin Mary known
as soon as the war would be over. Rome, aware of the findings as well as of the episcopal decision to delay approval,
thought that it would be in the spiritual interest of suffering
Belgium, to make approval known as soon as possible. Did
Rome take matters into its own hands, and start to act 'over
the head of the local Bishop', as the Garabandalists of today
are clamouring?

This is what took place:

"The new Bishop received from Rome a decree dated
December 7, 1942, and approved by Pope Pius XII, which
granted him *full liberty to proceed* toward canonical recognition.

On February 2nd, 1943, *the Bishop* published a Decree
which authorised public devotions to Our Lady of
Beauraing. This was during the dark days of the German
occupation of Belgium, and the people took great comfort
from this development ..." (From, *The Woman Shall Con-
quer*, by Don Sharkey.)

Note that Rome did not give the local Bishop *permission*
to proceed with the canonical recognition, but advised him
to make full use of his liberty to *proceed now*. If the Bishop
found it prudent to wait until after the war, to prevent up-
setting the Germans with 'unlawful gatherings', etc. at the
shrine, then Rome wanted him to reconsider in the light of
pressing spiritual needs. The joy of Our Lady's concern was

not meant only for the people of Belgium in those dark days, but for the whole Church.

3. We must not assume that 'Garabandal' is a moving story of devotion and innocence, only to be squashed by bishops 'who have a vested interest in squashing these things'. The Garabandal story discredits itself. One of the most revolting and offensive parts is "The 'miracle' of the visible host". Here the deceit becomes very ugly and sinister indeed. I will tell the story in the words of two of the most recommended authors on the topic, so I do not stand accused of 'making it up', or making it sound more terrible than it is.

The Apparitions of Garabandal, by F. Sanchez-Ventura Y Pascual, and *Our Lady comes to Garabandal,* by Joseph A. Pelletier.

The story of the miracle begins with Conchita inviting everybody to come along: "Hearing that the child was sending letters *all over the country* announcing the miracle ..." (p.125.)

Well they had the desired effect:

"The 18th of July (1962) came, and the streets of the hamlet were filled with a growing number of pilgrims and sight-seers ... Near Conchita's house a village dance was under way to the strains of bagpipes and drums ..." (p.125.) "It is estimated that between 2000 and 3000 people were in the village on that day ..." (p.107.)

The crowd behaved like any other mob:

"As she crossed the threshold, the crowd waiting before the house opened in just sufficient time to let her pass, and then the multitude was milling around her, like a river that had burst its banks and sweeps away everything in its path. I saw people falling to the ground and trampled by others. As far as I know, nobody was hurt. But the sight of that fantastic mob on the run, shoving and elbowing one another, *could not be more terrifying* … (p.129.) "I staunchly withstood the pushing of those behind me, striving with all my might not to be wrenched from my vantage point." (p.129-130. The amateur cameraman speaking.) "I only remember, as in a dream, voices crying out to me to get down, and I felt a heavy blow on my head …". (p.130. Same man.) "Seconds later, he was pushed violently, and fell to the ground with the camera …". (p.109.) [All this at 2 o'clock in the morning, mind you! But he managed to get his pictures, although absolutely unfamiliar with the use of a movie camera …]

Meanwhile, how did Conchita 'pose' for those shots?

"By 10 o'clock (pm) I had already received one call. At midnight, I received another. Then later, at 2 in the morning the Angel appeared to me in a room in my house …" (p.104.) "Conchita neglects to say in the Diary that some time after the start of the apparition, she engaged in one of her characteristic ecstatic marches. With her head flung back, she very quickly descended the stairs from her room on the 2nd floor where the vision had started. She passed out of the house into the expectant crowd which milled around her and followed her. She turned left around the corner of her house into a lane, and then left again into a street. There in the street, immediately behind her house she fell suddenly on her knees *in a puddle of water* and received visible communion from the angel …" p.106.) "I attempted to follow Conchita, but a crowd 15 or 20 foot deep separated us. [The hired cameraman speaking.] I sometimes caught a vague glimpse of her. She turned left along the lane formed by the side of her house and a low wall. She turned left again, and there, right in the middle of the alley, which is fairly wide at that spot, she suddenly fell to her knees. Her fall was so unexpected that the avalanche of people were carried past on either side of her by the weight of their own numbers. I was fortunate in not being carried past them, and before I knew it, I unexpectedly found myself to her right, *with her face a mere 18 inches from mine …*" (p.129.) [And in this nightmare were the only pictures taken by a self professed fumbler who knew nothing about camera handling, and who even forgot he had the camera until the very last moment …]

These, then, are the circumstances we are asked to believe that the Infinite Majesty of God had ordained from all Eternity, as the 'worthy' setting for a 'miracle' surrounding the Adorable Presence of His Son in the Blessed Eucharist, to prove the 'veracity' of the presence of the Mother of God in Garabandal …

- a wild and uncontrollable mob out for sensation,
- passing away the time with dancing,
- called there by the principle instigator,
- in the darkness of night, at 2 o'clock in the morning,
- in a dark alley,
- in a puddle of water …

If this is not a picture of 'the church of darkness', where deceit and confusion reign, nothing will be. And if we compare this me-lee with the dignity and reverence of Fatima (which it obviously is at pains to destroy), then we can understand how the young man and his mother were rapidly losing their love for Fatima, if they considered this a worthy substitute ...

Can we really see the Prefect of the Sacred Congregation for the Doctrine of the Faith bowing to pressure to give up everything he and the Church hold holy, and to override a Bishop who, in the execution of his God-given duty, condemned all this 'as having no Supernatural origin', in order to recommend *this* to us 'as having come from God'?

Finally, we can be sure of one thing: the expected 'miracle' will be of the same fraudulent character (if they can pull it off!) as this so-called 'miracle' described here, arranged to prove Garabandal true ...

Book II

The Victimhood of Our Blessed Lady

Frits Albers, Ph.B.

May, 1995

Part I

The New Eve

It is Catholic Doctrine that it has been divinely revealed by God that Our Blessed Lady's Assumption into Heaven was due to Her because of Her acceptance of Victimhood as the New Eve of the Redemption. For that was the way this latest Marian Dogma was traced by the defining Holy Father, Pope Pius XII, to the sources of Revelation in 1950. (See *Vatican II - Marian Council* by Rev. Fr.W.G. Most. ch. 5.) From this Dogmatic Teaching we will develop here the following theological thoughts which are at the Heart of the Marian Church:

"... the role of the Blessed Virgin in the Mystery of the Incarnate Word and the Mystical Body ..." (Second Vatican Council, *Lumen Gentium*, 54).

With these words the Council Fathers, assisted by the Holy Spirit, clearly indicate that they see the dual role played by Our Blessed Lady in the formation of the Human Body of Christ as well as His Mystical Body as two separate aspects of but *one* Mystery. Part of this Mystery, that is to say the great event that for one moment in history, at the Incarnation, the Mother of God was the Church, stood proxy for the whole Church, the Mystical Body of Christ, so that our Divine Saviour could save the world, including His Body the Church and His Holy Mother, *as the Head of that Body*, this Mystery is so full of consolation for us in our troubled times, that it warrants further investigation.

Pope Pius XII has infallibly taught us that this great union of Our Blessed Lady with the Church founded by Christ is a Mystery of our Catholic Faith, a Revealed Truth, to be believed by the whole Catholic Church as a Dogma of our Divine Faith. For it was on this great union that he founded the Dogma of Our Lady's Assumption into Heaven, body and soul. It was not the union between Mother and Son, but the inseparable union between Body and Head, between the New Eve and the New Adam, which finally became the vehicle by which the Dogma of the Assumption was traced to the sources of Revelation. Mary did not only freely cooperate with Her Divine Son as best She could, no, She provided the one essential element that had been hidden for all ages in the unsearchable depths of the Decree of God's Wisdom: that His Son would save the world as the Head of His Body the Church. At the Incarnation, and later, on Calvary, She provided that Body ...

St. Paul knew it:

"Such is the richness of the grace which He has showered on us in all Wisdom and insight. He has let us know the mystery of His purpose, the hidden plan He so kindly made in Christ from the beginning, to act upon when the times had run their course to the end: that He would bring everything together under Christ *as Head*, everything in the Heavens and on earth". (Eph. 1:7-10. See also Rom. 16:25; Gal. 4:4; Col. 1:16-20, esp. 18; etc.)

With the obvious meaning: as the Head of a Body, identified by St. Paul as His Church; not as a Head without a Body!

St. Paul knew after the great mystery had been revealed in Christ. How did Our Lady know beforehand? Before delving into this truly fascinating question it would be most appropriate if we could first acquire a more thorough appreciation of the doctrine of St. Paul as taught by Pope Pius XII in his Constitution *Munificentissimus Deus* of 1950, in which this great Pontiff not only declared for the whole Church the Dogma of Mary's Assumption into Heaven, but also traced for us the roots of this Dogma to the sources of Revelation. Much space of the first 38 numbers of this magnificent document was devoted to a review of 1900 years of teaching on the Assumption by the Fathers and Doctors of the Church.

Exalting this unanimous belief of Tradition: how proper and fitting Mary's Assumption is, as the voice of the Holy Spirit, the Holy Father broke new ground in No. 39 to give this universal Faith of the Church the solid foundation in Revelation it still required. I shall first provide you here with the full translation of that famous number 39:

"We must remember especially that since the Second Century the Virgin Mary has been designated by the holy Fathers as the New Eve who, though subject to the New Adam, is most intimately associated with Him in that struggle against the infernal foe which, as was foretold in the Proto-Evangelium, would finally result in that most complete victory over Sin and Death, which are always mentioned together in the writings of the Apostle of the Gentiles. Consequently, just as the glorious Resurrection of Christ was an essential part and the final sign of this victory, so that struggle which was common to the Blessed Virgin Mary and Her Divine Son had to be brought to a close by the glorification of Her virginal body. For it is the same Apostle who says: When this mortal thing hath put on immortality, then shall come to pass the saying that is written: 'Death is swallowed up in victory'." (1 Cor. 15:54)

In his beautiful book *Vatican II - Marian Council*, the author Fr. William Most in his brief commentary on this text calls the thought of Pope Pius XII here both brilliant and difficult, the latter mainly because it is so closely knitted. The full force of the papal teaching springs to light from the Latin text: "the glorification of Her virginal body *had to follow!*" By necessity. And on what did the Holy Father place this necessity? On only *one* thing: on a *common struggle!* "*that struggle which was common to the Blessed Virgin Mary and Her Divine Son*".

In the first 38 numbers of his Constitution the Holy Father shows that he was well aware of all that which 1900 years of Tradition had taught on the Assumption of Our Blessed Lady. Mentioning and bypassing all the fitting reasons for Catholic belief in Our Lady's glorious Assumption, Pope Pius XII broke new ground in No. 39 where at last he came to the crux of the whole matter: on what facts, revealed in Revelation and contained in Sacred Scripture was this solemn doctrine founded, for it to be declared Revealed Truth, infallibly true?

The Dogma of Mary's Assumption body and soul into Heaven is not based by the defining Holy Father on any of Her privileges. It is not based on Her Immaculate Conception. Nor is it based on Her Divine Motherhood. It is really not based by the Pope on anything that God had done for Her: it is strictly speaking based on what Mary did for God! It is squarely based here by the defining Pontiff on Her absolutely free choice to go beyond the call of mere duty to that of *Victimhood*: to be the 'New Eve' with the 'New Adam' ... ! Let us see what stunning Revelation came out of that!

Part II

Doctrinal Foundations of the New Eve in Church Documents

I shall put before readers three of the highest Church documents to enlighten us on the Truth, declared here by the Holy Father to have been revealed by God: that the work of Redemption was so common to Our Blessed Lady and Her Son that, by necessity, a common or equal glory had to follow. Equal in kind, not in degree.

1. A first explanation is offered us in the next paragraph of the present document, in which the Holy Father states:

"Hence the revered Mother of God, *'from all eternity joined in a hidden way with Jesus Christ in one and the same Decree of Predestination'* ... finally obtained ... that She should be preserved free from the corruption of the tomb ..." (No 40).

The quoted words emphasised in this text were taken by His Holiness Pope Pius XII from the Bull *Ineffabilis Deus* in which his predecessor Pope Pius IX had declared and formulated the Dogma of the Immaculate Conception almost a century before, in 1854. They are weighty words, not used lightly by Our Holy Mother the Catholic Church.

We know from the words of St. Paul, quoted previously, that Christ in His human nature was predestined by a Divine Decree, hidden in God from all eternity:

    a. to be a Divine Person, united with the Word, the eternal Son of the Father and

    b. to be the Head of the Church, His Body, and so redeem the human race, to allow both His human and His Mystical Body to take part in that Redemption.

Here two Holy Fathers, almost a century apart, in two documents of the Church carrying supreme authority as they are dealing with two Marian Dogmas, in tracing these two Dogmas to the sources of Revelation have declared with the authority of Christ Himself, that Mary has a share in that Supreme Decree and was not only predestined (a) to be the Mother of God, but also (b) to be His Bride. To be the beginning of that other Body of Christ, His Mystical Body, of which Christ is the Head. And in consenting to both aspects of this same Decree of Predestination, two things happened:

    i. the infinite merits of Christ redeemed the whole world including His Mother, which was the role of the Head alone; and

    ii. the same infinite merits were placed at the disposal of His Body the Church for the salvation of 'the many' who would in time avail themselves of these graces: the role of the Head and His Mystical Body.

Only in that way could St. Paul write "that he was completing in his own body what was still lacking in the sufferings of Christ". (Col. 1:24).

Thus the great Sacrifice on Calvary became the Sacrifice of the *whole Church*, Head and Body. And because the Apostles had fled, Mary stood in, stood proxy, for the whole Church! Understanding the deep significance of the double aspect of this Eternal Decree and complying with it "*with all Her heart, with all Her soul, with all Her mind and with all Her strength*" (Mk. 12:30). And again we ask ourselves: How had She known? Not only on Calvary: how had She known right from the start? How come She had understood all along?

2. A second supreme document I had in mind to refer my readers to for further enlightenment on the profound Truth declared here by the Holy Father to have been revealed by God: that the work of the Redemption was so common to Our Lady and Her Divine Son, that by necessity an equal glory had to follow, is the Second Vatican Council's Constitution on the Sacred Liturgy. I once again hand you over to Fr. W. Most:

"The Vatican Council says in No. 10 that the Mass is the *renewal of the New Covenant. Now in the renewal there is, all* readily admit, a twofold offering: the offering of Christ the Head, to which is joined the offering of His members which we are. We really do join with Him in the offering of the Mass. So then, if the *renewal* is twofold, formed of the obedience of Christ to which is added that of His members, then would it not be strange if the *original* which the renewal repeats, did not have a similar twofold structure? Really if the renewal were two-fold, and the original not, then the renewal would be partly false, it would not repeat fully what it should repeat. Therefore the original must have been twofold: Mary's offering, Her obedience, must have fused with the obedient offering of Christ. His obedience as we saw was the price of the Redemption. Her obedience, said Vatican II, was joined with His. What else should that mean if not that She shared in paying the very price of the Redemption." (*Vatican II - Marian Council*, p. 26-27.)

It is precisely this sharing of the very price of the Redemption which is renewed and reflected by every Catholic Mass, for this sharing of the duties of being a Head, and of providing a Body so necessary to the Head, set in motion at the Annunciation, came to the fullest fruition on Calvary where "Mary's obedience was joined with His", just as joined disobedience in 'the head of the human race and his first body' had produced the Fall. Mary really does have power. Her offering is of *real* value, even if subordinate.

Knowingly and obediently She provided the Mystical Body Her Son needed as Head to comply with the Eternal Decree in the Blessed Trinity: to save the human race as the Head of a Body. And in that She is the beginning, the Mother and the Model of the Church, the other members of that Body He so desperately needs ... And long before St. Paul, She had already often prayed: "*I can do all things in Him Who strengthens me*", even providing My part in redeeming the world.

3. Can this be substantiated? Are these just nice theological opinions? Pious effusions squeezed from obscure doctrinal formulations? Or does all this lie so close to the fundamental Truths of our Supernatural existence in Christ and the Mystical Body, that it is the lifeblood of the very Church we profess to love and cherish? The supernatural air we breathe in even unwittingly if nevertheless necessarily? Let me take you to yet a third supreme document of the Church, the tail end of the encyclical letter of His Holiness Pope Pius XII: *The Mystical Body of Christ and our union in it with Christ*, 1943.

"Venerable Brethren, may the Virgin Mother of God hear the prayers of our paternal heart ... and obtain for all a true love of the Church; She whose sinless soul was filled with the divine Spirit of Jesus Christ above all other created souls, and who *'in the name of the whole human race'* gave Her consent *'for a spiritual marriage between the Son of God and human nature.'* (St. Thomas. Summa Theol. I II, q.30, a.1, c.). <u>Within Her virginal womb</u> Christ our Lord already bore the exalted title of <u>Head of the Church</u>. In a marvellous birth She brought Him forth as the source of all Supernatural Life, and presented Him newly born as Prophet, King and Priest to those who, from among the Jews and the Gentiles, were the first to come to adore Him ... It was She, the second Eve, who, free from all sin, original or personal, and always most intimately united with Her Son, <u>offered Him on Golgotha</u> to the Eternal Father for all the children of Adam, and Her mother's <u>rights</u> and Her mother's love were included in the holocaust. Thus She who, according to the flesh, was the Mother of our Head, through the added title of pain and glory became according to the Spirit, the Mother of all His members .... bearing with courage and confidence the tremendous burden of Her sorrows and desolation. She, truly the Queen of

Martyrs, more than all the faithful '*made up what was still lacking in the sufferings of Christ for His Body the Church*' [Col. 1:24]. And She continues to have for the Mystical Body of Christ, born of the pierced Heart of the Saviour, the same motherly care and ardent love with which She cherished and fed the Infant Jesus in the crib." (No. 110).

This leaves in clarity nothing to be desired. It spells out all we still wished to know for certain. If it is Catholic teaching that Christ already in the womb of His Mother carried the exalted title of *Head of a Mystical Body*, then that Body must have already been in existence, and could only have come into existence by the consent of His Mother. This shows that Our Lady, already at the time of the Annunciation, had a profound grasp of what St. Paul has revealed had been hidden for all ages in the unsearchable depths of God's Wisdom: the Divine Decree that Christ was predestined to be the Son of God, and that He would save the world in union with others, i.e. as the Head of His Body the Church, even if the grace of that union, and the grace of participation with it, depended entirely on the fullness of Grace in Him, the Head!

The acceptance of this grace and the inherent and subsequent obedience of full cooperation with it were made, according to Papal teaching here, by Our Blessed Lady "in name of the whole human race", presented here under the image of a sacred and unbreakable marriage vow.

If we realise that Mary stood proxy for the whole Church on Calvary after the Apostles had fled, to provide Christ our Head with the Mystical Body He needed for the Redemption of the whole human race, then we know now for certain where the understanding and acceptance of this sacred vow had its beginning in His holy Mother!

What thinking had brought Mary to the threshold of this Mystery so that, when the Revelation of it came to Her at the time of the Annunciation, it found Her willing and prepared to understand and to accept not only that the Son of God wished to be Her Son but also wanted to be Her Head? Christ, materially speaking, could have taken flesh out of any woman, but who but the Blessed Virgin Mary would have possessed the superabundance of love needed to provide Him *from Her own existence* with a suffering body that He needed under a suffering Head?

This question is on a par with the degree of difficulty He has experienced over the centuries of finding for Himself Christians who so fully understood and loved Him and His saving work, that they were willing and prepared to be victims under a suffering Head and not just anyone sheltering under the name 'Christian'!

Our Lady is the sealed fountain known only to God. But She is pleased to unfold Her treasures and graces to any of Her children who love and revere Her. One of those rare pearls is a ray of light into the prayerlife of our Blessed Mother, light from Heaven on Her meditations on the Old Testament text, by means of which the Holy Spirit of God guided Her to the future revelation of His Divine Decrees ...

Part III

The Prayer Life of the Blessed Virgin

The prayerlife of the Blessed Virgin Mary ... Who but the most pure can ever hope to gain access to it, unless we all have been asked by invitation? Have we been invited? Two Popes have declared that Our Blessed Lady was so intimately joined to Her Son that there was but one and the same Decree of Predestination involving them both. If She was, and if it has been revealed to us, that this divine Decree consisted of two distinct parts, then Our Lady must have known the full extent of that union in order to give Her consent.

And when, on another occasion, one of these two Holy Fathers has declared that already in Her sacred womb Christ was present there as the Head of His Church, then we understand that this could only be because He had found a Body fitted for such a Head. And who but Our Blessed Mother could have given Him that Body?

At that time there was no St. Peter, no St. Paul, no St. John. The only one who could have been the Church for such a Head was the one who must have had full knowledge of the totality of that Decree at the time of the Annunciation and had accepted every aspect of it, when in obedience to that Decree She gave Her consent to the Incarnation. The Council Fathers were right: to provide the Son of God with a human as well as with a mystical body appears as the two aspects of but one Mystery, as the two halves of but one Decree of Predestination.

And with such revelations and pronouncements Mary's mystical life has been incorporated into the prayerlife of the Church, and have we indeed been encouraged by the Holy Catholic Church to enter into that intimate domain in order to understand for our own benefit how our heavenly Mother was led by the Sacred Scriptures and by the Holy Spirit to the threshold of the revelation of this fathomless Decree, and to Her acceptance of all that it entailed "*in name of Herself and of the whole human race*".

Encouraged by considerations such as these let us look then in some detail to the actual wording in which some of those Mysteries contemplated by Our Blessed Lady are veiled. Unencumbered by modern attempts to make the Bible say what the various translators think the Bible ought to say, or what they wish the Bible had said, Mary's perception of the Word of God was pure and direct, not wrapped in any additional veil imposed on the text by human interference. This is no idle remark. We know e.g. that Our Blessed Lady read Eve's words in Gen.4:1 in the Hebrew text as "*I have gotten a man, Yahweh.*" To Her penetrating understanding of the impression the Fall and the Promise had made on our first parents, these words were perfectly natural, even if Eve was mistaken in thinking that Yahweh had already fulfilled His Promise.

Although premature (as we know from hindsight) these words of Eve were there, inserted by the Holy Spirit for a meaning beyond human understanding. And so for Our Lady these words stood, and would one day have the meaning the Holy Spirit had given them!

Thus in tracing Our Blessed Lady's meditations on the Word of God in order to catch a glimpse of Her supernatural insights, we cannot be guided by mere human attempts even at mitigating the starkness of a difficult text, let alone at making the Word of God mean what Modernism and other corruptions of the human and Catholic mind wish it to mean by simply rejecting or rewriting what seems unacceptable to the follies of those minds.

Yet, to appreciate the trigger point in Our Lady's mind, the threshold, where advanced human thinking cannot go any further until it is lifted up by God's Revelation into participation in the Act of Divine Thinking: to become, in other words, an act of Infused, Divine and Supernatural Faith, Eve's words are central and indispensable! Many Jews knew about the intimate relationship between Yahweh, personally coming to the aid of His people, and His suffering Servant. But not even in their wildest dreams would it ever occur to them that these Two would be the one and same Person, that the Suffering Servant would be more than human: that in fact He would be God!. That one day a certain Woman would truthfully exclaim Eve's words: "*I have gotten a man: God*".

When it was revealed to Her by the Angel Gabriel that there are Three Persons in God, a Trinity of Persons in the one and undivided Godhead, only then did the most advanced of all human thinking accept the Truth in the Supernatural Light of Faith, that the Second Person of this Blessed Trinity wanted to be Her Son, and so enabled Her to say at last in all truthfulness what Eve had prematurely exclaimed in Her honour: "*I have gotten a Man, God!*". Only then did it occur to Mary how Yahweh Himself could be the suffering Servant, coming to the aid of His people, and how good people everywhere could rally to His cause.

And so the finer points of the Old Testament came to the notice of the prayerful Mary "and were pondered by Her in Her Immaculate Heart". There is, all will agree, a distinct difference between a general willingness to cooperate, and the specific generosity to obey a certain way in which God wants this cooperation to take place. For all ages there had been hidden in God a Decree which had predestined that His Son would have Two Bodies; that He would redeem the human race not only in His human body, as a human Individual, though not as a human person, but also as the Head of a corporate Body of other human individuals, which collectively had been foretold by God in Paradise as "*the Seed of the Woman*".

Scattered throughout the Old Testament in the Messianic part of the Sacred Text, these valuable references begin the first outline of the Church, which, as the Body of the Head, had been made by that Divine Decree just as indispensable as the Head itself. Due to the prompting of the Holy Spirit, these valuable clues had not escaped the penetrating power of the prayerful Mary. Lying in Her heart and mind at the threshold of human understanding, they there awaited the graciousness of God to be lifted beyond themselves into the cohesion of God's everlasting knowledge.

1. Mary had read and pondered about texts such as these:

- "Thine O Lord is the greatness and the power and the glory and the victory and the majesty; for all that is in the heavens and in the earth is thine; thine is the kingdom, O Lord, and thou art exalted as head above all." [1 Chr. 29:11]. And:

- "Thou didst deliver Me from strife with the peoples; thou didst keep Me as the head of the nations; people whom I had not known served Me." [2 Sam. 22:44], which is substantially the same as Ps. 18:43, in which texts the joy of the Psalmist is expressed over the fact that the future Deliverer will be the Head of the New Creation.

But here, as in so many other texts which are truly Messianic, what is being said about the Messiah has previously been said about Yahweh. The all-time classic is, of course, what Christ Himself threw up at His adversaries: "If David can call Him 'Lord', how can He be his Son?" (The Lord, Yahweh, said to my Lord, the Messiah ...)

In the first of the two texts I have quoted here, the Lord God is called the Head, and in the second one, it is the Messiah on whom this unique title is being bestowed. The awareness of the closeness of this wondrous relationship between Yahweh and His Messiah in a prayerful life as that of the Blessed Virgin Mary was of course a source of great joy and consolation, but, as remarked before, not until the Revelation of the existence of the Trinity of Persons in the one Godhead, could the true relationship be believed and understood.

2. If the Headship of the future Redeemer was revealed by God in the Old Dispensation, what about texts which refer to the Body belonging to such a Head? Even in this we do not find the Old Testament wanting in clarity. Does not the author of

the Letter to the Hebrews quote the Psalmist in ch. 10, vs. 5-7 with the words:

"You, who wanted no sacrifice or oblation, prepared a body for Me. You took no pleasure in holocausts or sacrifices for sin; then I said, just as I was commanded in the scroll of the book: 'God, here am I! I have come to do Your Will'."

And we can hear Our Blessed Lady meditate:

If it goes without saying for any intelligent creature to acknowledge before God that his or her body comes from the Creator, why is it so special for the Messiah to mention this fact? Who might He be, this Messiah? Did He not have a body beforehand?

Moreover, would it be possible to come across some texts anywhere in Sacred Scripture which would substantiate that the Messiah, in addition to referring here to His Human Body, could also have been pointing beyond this body to another Body, that Corporate Body which He requires as Head? For Head He had been ordained to be. Without a shadow of a doubt the Holy Spirit would have directed the deep, prayerful attention of His future Bride to that wonderful part of the Old Testament, the Song of Songs, from whose scented pages the lyrics, extolling the desire of the beloved for his bride, reveal the ardour, almost the pain, of the Messiah, once He appeared in the flesh, to be united with His Bride, His very own Church, to become one body with her. A body that would share with Him whatever the 'New Eve', the 'Woman of the Promise', would have to suffer with the 'New Adam' from 'the seed of the serpent'.

Part IV

The Annunciation and The Incarnation

And so, when the Archangel Gabriel appeared to Her and explained it all to Her, Mary was ready. When it was revealed to Her that there is a Trinity in God; that the Son of the Most High wanted to be Her Son; and when, at Her request, it was explained to Her that this would be the work of the Third Person in the adorable Trinity, the Holy Spirit, Mary obeyed. She not only allowed the Son of God to take His human Body from Hers, but, understanding His ardent desire to be united with the human race as its Head, She also provided Him in Her own existence with the beginning of that other Body, His Mystical Body, in order that He could do what had been predestined and hidden in God from all ages: to save the human race as the Head of a corporate Body, His Church.

Thus it was that a future Vicar of this Eternal Head of that Church could truthfully declare in one of his encyclicals: "that already in Mary's womb, Christ was the Head of His Church". For He had not only been fitted with a Body that made Him human, but also with a Body that made Him Head.

The greatness of Mary is not only found in this that She, fully aware from Sacred Scripture that the Mystical Body She was asked to provide for the Son of God from Her own existence, would have to suffer as much as His Human Body, nevertheless submitted to the Eternal Decree on behalf of Herself. Her greatness came to perfection when She also dared to accept on behalf of Her children, Her other seed, who in time would extend this Suffering Body to the four corners of the globe, and so share in Her glory. This way She became not only the beginning of this Church, but also its Mother and Model. For, at one distinct moment in time, She *was* that Church, standing in for all of us, in union with Her Head.

From that moment on no church could claim to be the true Body of Christ in dissociation from Her, i.e. not modeled on Her, as is the case with all the Protestant churches. And that will also be the flaw in the modern, ecumenical church of darkness. For, no matter how hard the Modernists and Teilhardians work to make their church of darkness "look like the Lamb": not being created in the image and likeness of the Lamb's Holy Mother, it will always "speak like the Dragon".

From that one moment in history onwards, when She stood proxy for all of us, no 'church' can supplement (not even its social teaching) by borrowing from Communism and claim to be the Catholic Church. For, if the fullness of the true Church was found at one stage in the Union between the New Adam and the New Eve, then we can only, as children, live from that fullness. We can neither augment it nor pretend that it is lacking in essentials!

It is thanks to Mary that now every Christian can repeat what Christ said coming into this world: "A Body thou hast fitted Me." God has fitted us with a human body and He has prepared for us the Mystical Body. And with the prayers and good works and sufferings in our own bodies, offered up in every Mass in union with Christ's Mystical Body, we can extend the benefits of that Other Body to the ends of the earth.

Thus Mary's meditations on Sacred Scripture led Her to the fullness of Faith in the Incarnation and to the understanding of

God's inscrutable Decree of how Redemption and the fullness of Grace in the Head Jesus were to be passed by His Body, the other seed of the Woman of Genesis, to the rest of the whole human race. For just as human beings possess the faculty of passing on Adam's Sin, the Sin of the head of the human race, by sexual propagation, so do the members of the Mystical Body of Christ have the power to pass on Grace from the Head of the New Creation. And for the Holy Church Our Blessed Lady is the Key to the full understanding of how this is done. For in Her we see how we must show our own union to the Head in much suffering and praying; in obedience and victimhood; in superabundance of love and good works for our fellow men. And in standing in for others until they too understand, as was once done for us by our Holy Mother Mary and by the Church.

"*Scripture has locked everything under Sin*" (Gal. 3:221). But Christ has unlocked for us this great "*Mystery of Iniquity*", (2 Thes.2:7), and has shown us how His Grace and forgiveness are passed on from Him, the Head, through His Mystical Body to the members of that Body first, and so flowing out to the whole human race to undo the ravages of Original Sin. It is at all times the prerogative of the head of the body to do the thinking. It is the privilege of the body to put the results of this thinking into practice in union with the head.

And the Key used by Christ to reveal to us the inestimable privilege of carrying out His thinking in the Mystical Body is the One whose work was so common with His, that at the Incarnation She fused with Him into the one Mystical Body by the one and the same Decree of Predestination for us, Her children. To create for the Head a virginal Church, pure and undefiled, "without spot or wrinkle", (Eph. 5:27), no matter how stained and defiled we Her children would ever be ...

It was necessary to trace the origins of Victimhood to Our Blessed Lady ahead to that of Her Son because chronologically speaking, it was understood and accepted by Our Heavenly Mother first, before Her Son made His appearance on earth. In fact it was Her understanding of Victimhood and Her acceptance of it that finally brought Him down here with us in the first place! For only in Her Victimhood could the Obedience be found necessary for the Incarnation.

But of course, all Victimhood, including that of Our Blessed Lady, can only fuse with the divine example of it, given us by the Son of God Himself. He could only inspire in His Heavenly Mother what had already been decreed - and accepted - from all eternity by God: that the human race was to be redeemed by a suffering Human Body as well as by a Suffering Mystical Body ... *both* to be provided for the Son of God by His own Mother, and from Her own substance, and *both* to be passed on to the One True Church, i.e. the Church created in the image and likeness of Mary: the *Marian* Church.

What does all this mean for us in the circumstances of our Catholic family lives at the end of the Second Millennium since all the foregoing had taken place? What is our reaction to Our Blessed Lady's Victimhood, embraced for us with so much love?

There is really no escape for us: the Head of the Mystical Body, the Church, is a crucified Man; and the beginning of that Church is a Virgin Mother, whose soul was pierced with a sword.

If, contemplating the vastness of it all and the implications it holds for us, we have difficulty in coming to grips with it, we may better understand the command God gave to Noah at the time of the great Flood: *"Build thee an Ark ..."*. In order never to go under we must build ourselves an Ark to float always on top of the deluge of sin that has again engulfed the whole world. And that Ark can only be a great love for Our Lady who will see to it that we remain in Communion with God and with His Church, that is, with each other. It will mean many privations of all the things that a lost world holds so dear: good health, wealth, comfort, popularity, esteem, a good name, all the things Noah did not have in the eyes of his mocking world, things he could not take with him in his ark, things we cannot take with us into our Ark.

In our state of victimhood, we are reminded of what Our Blessed Lord held up with such insistence to His Apostles:

"... because, I tell you, these words of Scripture must be fulfilled in Me: *'He let Himself be taken for a criminal'*." (Lk. 22:37.)

"Blessed are you when people hate you, drive you out, abuse you, denounce your name as criminal on account of the Son of Man. Rejoice when that day comes and *dance* for joy, for then your reward will be great in heaven." (Lk. 6:22-23.)

"Now keep this carefully in mind: *you are not to prepare your defence*, because I Myself shall give you an eloquence and a wisdom that none of your opponents will be able to resist or contradict." (Lk. 21:15.)

In the safety of our Ark, a great love for Our Lady, we can even dispense with the expense on our own behalf of engaging the services of drowning lawyers and barristers ...

But, although on divine command, even these professionals cannot take care of us here on earth, where everything nowadays is geared to consensus, there are of course very effective means in existence within the shelter of our Ark, by which we can take care of the eternal salvation of opponents and lawyers alike.

These means are spelled out in two of my recent books: *The Catholic Mass*, and *The Divine Art of Praying*.

Book III

The Glories of the New Eve

Frits Albers, Ph.B.

Originally Published
October, 1990

On the Feast of the Holy Rosary

Foreword

The most remarkable feature of the whole Modernist onslaught is, that no aspect of it was ever claimed to be presented to Catholicism in the name of the Most Holy Virgin Mary. The Modernists have been ceaselessly at pains to prove to us that their heresies can be traced to Vatican II, that they have the backing of Popes, and even that their 'parallel magisterium' must be accepted with the authority from God Himself for the good of the Church! Yet the 'Everlasting Enmity' established in Genesis by God 'between the Woman and Her Seed' on the one side, and 'you and your seed' on the other, still proves to be the insurmountable obstacle preventing any modern 'seed of Satan' from giving credibility to their claim, that the sewer of Modernism was unleashed on the Church in the name of God, as the preposterous claim that it was unleashed in the Name of the Blessed Virgin Mary.

It is true that in Tasmania a feeble attempt was made in 1990 to enforce RENEW on the Archdiocese of Hobart with a veneer of Marian piety, but the revolt of the true Marian Tradition of the Holy Catholic Church in this part of the world was so intense and spontaneous, that soon the enforcers of the program had to resort to their usual dislike for anything truly Catholic to show that even the origin of the Tasmanian RENEW was undiluted Modernism. Going by correspondence received, by private remarks made, and by public utterances delivered from the pulpit during the various RENEW campaigns, it is obvious that many RENEWED Catholics fail to see in the Blessed Virgin Mary anything more than an ordinary woman. Amongst these people the Protestant conviction is growing, expressed several times on paper, "that any woman could have been taken by God and could have fulfilled the role played by the Blessed Virgin Mary". Just as in those same minds the conviction is growing that 'any woman can be ordained a priest'. That explicit pronouncements such as these with regard to the Virgin Mother of God are on a par with a simple rejection of the Catholic Dogma of the Immaculate Conception, fails to arouse any great concern in these Catholics, showing to what darkness the 'Melbourne Guidelines for Religious Education' and freedom in sexual matters have reduced the Catholic Faith in our (young) Catholic adults and children.

If it is true that behind every theological problem there lurks first and foremost a moral problem, then the visible break-down of Marian <u>theology</u> and piety in Catholic hearts and minds reveals an invisible collapse of Catholic <u>morality</u> in those same minds and hearts and lives. The widespread use of artificial means of contraception has taken its toll and the sheep are paying dearly for the silence and encouragement they received from the local shepherds.

Only one Church was ever created by God in the image and likeness of His Holy Mother. It is that Church of which it has been written:

"In the liturgy the Church salutes Mary of Nazareth as the Church's own beginning ... Her fullness designates the hidden beginning of the Church's journey." (Redemptorist Mater 1987, #1. See also ## 20, 21, 38, 45 and 48.)

No one can claim to enforce with God's authority, or to impose in His Name, what he or she had not first received from this unique Daughter and this unique Mother. For the Holy Father continues:

"Thus, in Her New Motherhood in the Spirit, Mary embraces each and everyone IN the Church, and embraces each and everyone THROUGH the Church" (Ibid. #47.)

This has always been unalloyed Catholic teaching and is as true today as it was before Vatican II. Only one Church, the one "in and through which the Mother of God embraces each and every other human being" is the unique Church necessary for salvation. That is the only Church created in Her own spotless image and likeness; the One, Holy, Catholic and Apostolic Church, headed by the successor of Peter, the Rock on which this Church was founded and built.

For Catholics who still rejoice with great intensity in the fact that the Everlasting Enmity between our Blessed Lady and Satan still extends undiminished to our days and beyond, for those who attend to their daily duty in the glorious sunlight that no modern clap-trap can be forced on their Catholic Faith as coming from the Holy Church, because of the everlasting certainty that it could never be presented to them as coming from the Blessed Virgin Mary; those who appreciate the enormous preparation undertaken by God in human history prior to the Incarnation of His only-begotten Son, and who believe with their Mother, the Holy Catholic Church, that the Blessed Virgin Mary is truly the Mediatrix of all graces: for those unique Catholics the divine consolation contained in the Old Testament Wisdom literature is meant.

Readers of this little book presented herewith in the form of a 'Novena of Quotations' from the Wisdom literature of the Old Testament will soon realise that it is the author's joy to make available to a wider readership how, under the guidance of the Holy Spirit, Catholic Tradition from its Apostolic roots had used this Wisdom literature, inspired by the same infallible Spirit of God, to enrich the Church's understanding of the glories and privileges of the Blessed Virgin Mary, and so to enrich also the Church's understanding of Her own Marian roots.

That Church teaching and Catholic theology are safe guides on such a tour through an exquisite garden of Marian piety will be explained in the following Introduction and will be kept to the fore in the remainder of the book.

Introduction

In the Introduction to his 'Treatise on True Devotion', St. Louis Marie Grignion de Montfort makes the following statement of the Blessed Virgin Mary:

"So deep was her humility that her most powerful and unwavering desire throughout her whole life, was to remain hidden from herself and from all men, in order that she might be known to God alone."

Strong words. To single out this particular inclination in the Blessed Virgin Mary as "her most powerful and unwavering desire", can only come to a Saint after much prayer and meditation. Then, after a brief description on how the most Holy Trinity had respected this ardent desire throughout the life of the Mother of God on earth, the Saint reveals his own intentions to make Our Lady universally known and loved with these words:

"My aim is to show that Mary has been but very imperfectly known until now, and that this is one of the reasons why Jesus Christ is not known as He deserves to be known. When therefore, as is certain, the reign of Jesus Christ begins in this world, this will be as a necessary consequence of the knowledge and the reign of the Most Blessed Virgin."

Is St. Louis de Montfort a safe guide? As stated in the Foreword, only the Church can tell us for sure. Not only did she canonize St. Louis de Montfort in 1947, but in the Marian encyclical *Redemptorist Mater*, opening the 1987 Marian Year, the Saint was held up to the Universal Church by the author of the encyclical, Pope John Paul II with these words:

"In this regard (of historical Marian spirituality) I would like to recall among the many witnesses and teachers of this spirituality the figure of St. Louis Marie Grignion de Montfort, who proposes consecration to Christ through the hands of Mary as an effective means to live faithfully ones Baptismal commitment ... There thus exist solid points of reference to look to <u>and to follow</u> in the context of this Marian Year" (#48)

In the same encyclical the Holy Father explains what he means by the expression 'solid points of reference' when he wrote the following about the Mother of the Redeemer:

"Her exceptional pilgrimage in Faith represents a constant point of reference for the Church: for individuals and for communities, for peoples and nations, and in a sense for all humanity. It is indeed difficult to encompass and measure its range." (#6)

What the Holy Father means with these words of all inclusive importance, – what he calls – 'Marian Dimension', he develops throughout the entire encyclical, e.g.:

"In the liturgy the Church salutes Mary of Nazareth as the Church's own beginning ... Her fullness designates the hidden beginning of the Church's journey." (#1) See also (#20), (#21), (#38), (#45), (#48).

"Through the Mystery of Christ she too is present within mankind." (#19)

"Thus, in Her New Motherhood in the Spirit, Mary embraces each and everyone IN the Church, and embraces each and everyone THROUGH the Church" (#47.)

"Knowledge of the true Catholic doctrine regarding the Blessed Virgin Mary will always be a key to the exact understanding of the Mystery of Christ and the Church. The Church must draw from the Virgin Mother of God the most authentic form of perfect imitation of Christ." (#47). (Here the Holy Father quotes the words of his predecessor Pope Paul VI, 1964.)

Thus, having heard the Church's doctrine on Our Blessed Lady being singled out by the Holy Father as 'the constant reference point' for all, in order that each may come to a sure understanding 'of the Mystery of Christ and of the Church', we note that the Pope uses the same terminology, 'solid points of reference' in connection with the spiritual legacy of St. Louis de Montfort. We may therefore conclude that, in the mind of the Holy Father, the ideal of St. Louis' 'True Devotion', if properly lived, is bound to open one's mind to the so desirable 'knowledge of the true Catholic doctrine regarding the Blessed Virgin Mary', the key to the exact understanding of the 'Mystery of Christ and of the Church', making the Saint a sure guide. Thus, if with a slight variation, we wish to repeat the above quoted words of St. Louis as follows,

"My aim is to show that Mary has been but very imperfectly known until now, and that this is one of the reasons why the True Catholic Church of Jesus Christ, the one He created in the image and likeness of His Holy Mother, is not known and loved as this Holy Church deserves to be known and loved."

then we are not alone, neither in our concern nor in our wish to remedy the situation, as the Holy Father as late as 1987 distinctly declared that "knowledge of the true Catholic doctrine regarding

the Blessed Virgin Mary will always be a key to the exact understanding of the Mystery ... of the Church". (RM #47)

How accurate this teaching is springs immediately to light if it
is further realised that two Holy Fathers, Pope Pius IX and Pope
Pius XII, on the occasion of two dogmatic definitions concerning
the Blessed Virgin Mary, Her Immaculate Conception in 1854 and
Her Assumption in 1950, have stated "that Mary is in the same Decree of Predestination as the Son of God". Only with these words
will it begin to imprint itself on our minds how necessary the
teaching of Tradition on the Blessed Virgin Mary is for the true
understanding of the 'Mystery of the Church', and that the glib,
Modernist conviction 'that any other woman could have done for
the job' is nothing but an atrocious heresy, defying logic and Dogma, that is, Divine Revelation! For these solemn words, enshrined
in two Dogmas of the Church, "that Mary is in the same Decree of
Predestination as the Son of God", have never been said of any
other woman, and can be truthfully said only of one: "The Woman
of Genesis", the "New Eve", "Mary of Nazareth", "the Church's
own beginning". And it is to the everlasting glory of the Virgin
Mother of God, that this Church took its beginning in Her through
Her free consent, not only to become the Mother of God, but also
His Bride, His 'New Eve', the beginning of His Mystical Body in
time, His very own Church.

This unbreakable link with the Blessed Virgin Mary makes the
True Church of Jesus Christ unique. Any Catholic rejecting devotion to Our Lady as an integral part of the Church's life, any Catholic that is who "chases the Woman into the desert" of oblivion
(Rev. 12: 14), has sought and obtained admission into a strange

'church', which Christ will not recognize as the one founded by Him, 'as the Name of His Mother is not indelibly engraved on the pillars of its (so called) sanctuary'. (Rev. 3:12)

As we have been assured, the Blessed Trinity respected the ardent wish of Mary to be known only to God. Yet, Divine Wisdom also knows what an irresistible attraction to personal holiness is even a mere glimpse of the exquisite graces bestowed on the soul of this privileged creature, as is the growing awareness of the unique way in which She responded to God's largesse. And divine wisdom found a way out of the impasse. No one but God could reveal, as also no one but the Holy Spirit could inspire the writing down of His revelation in such a way that, at the same time, it would also conceal.

Thus He became the Author of the 'Books of Wisdom', rejected by Jews and Protestants alike, and so the sole property of that One Uniquely True Church that would one day glory in their possession, as She would in the fact of having been created in the image and likeness of Her whose glories lie revealed under the veil of Wisdom.

In several places in the Wisdom Books the sacred authors make it clear that they are writing about 'created wisdom'. After the Incarnation this refers also to the human wisdom of Christ. And it is here that the genius of the Holy Spirit comes into full view. Nowhere is it ever stated that Our Blessed Lady ever acted on Her own. Of Her it is written:

"From the moment of the Annunciation and conception Mary followed Jesus step by step in Her maternal pilgrimage of Faith." (RM #26) as, in Her sinless way, She had obeyed God's Will up till then in every detail. Yet, in order that the wisdom of Our Lady could be a legitimate contribution to the wisdom of Christ and, as the wisdom of the 'New Eve', could fuse with the wisdom of the 'New Adam', to become the <u>one</u> wisdom of the Holy Church, (just as the absence of wisdom in Eve 'fused' with the rejection of wisdom by Adam, to become the <u>one</u> darkness of Original Sin in all humanity), Mary's wisdom is a cherished pearl on its own. And it is this inheritance, the glory of the Church, which lies revealed in the Wisdom Books as a separate entity yet bathed in the glow of the Wisdom of Christ.

Or looked at somewhat differently again, just as a statue of Our Lady is carved (or ought to be!) in the human form of a most chaste and beautiful woman in order that it can act as the most appropriate 'veil' by means of which we come, through Faith, into contact with the unique but unseen personality behind it, so the Holy Spirit has chosen for us, in the manifold glories of the virtue of Wisdom, a most beautiful and unique reality by means of which His adopted sons and daughters can come into contact with Her, through whose wise consent they have come to share in Her exalted state. And just as devotion to Our Lady always leads one to Christ, (and a great devotion to Our Lady leads to a great union with God), so the legitimate delight in the manifold glories of Wisdom in the Old Testament, inspiring great love for the Blessed Virgin Mary, will only be a beginning of an ever deeper penetration into the Wisdom of Christ: "the Wisdom of the Cross". For such are the safeguards built into the sacred text by uncreated Wisdom itself, that if the unction that exudes from the hallowed pages does not lead to great union with God in ALL truth, the text will remain a closed book and will not lead to anything, as there is no such thing as a 'half-truth'. Thus if by the wish of the Holy Spirit the Wisdom Books of the Old Testament inspire a great love for the Blessed Virgin Mary, and for the Church created in Her sacred image and likeness, they ought to inspire an even greater love and deeper gratitude for the Wisdom of the One Triune God 'Who created Her'. (Si. 1:9)

I

"The Lord possessed me in the beginning of His ways"

The Holy Catholic Church, headed by the Vicar of Christ on earth, the Pope, Bishop of Rome, is the sole instrument willed by God and founded by His Son on earth, Our Lord and Saviour Jesus Christ, for the salvation of all mankind. This means that all graces for the salvation of every human being flow exclusively through this Church into the whole world. This age-old article of Faith, formulated from earliest times in the phrase: "Outside the Church there is no salvation" has from times immemorial meant that 'outside the Catholic Church, and the Catholic Faith within Her, there are no other means of salvation'. Even Protestants, when they safely land on the shores of Paradise, will find with intense gratitude that ultimately their salvation did not depend on their defective 'christian faith', but on the endless flow of sanctifying graces poured out over humanity from the fullness of Christ within the Catholic Church, acclaimed by Catholic Faith.

No wonder that Satan, in his final and global onslaught on the effectiveness of this Holy Church, is presently using his most diabolical 'seed': Modernism and the Modernists, to launch his all-out war on this rare pearl of absolute value: the Holy Catholic Faith. For, after two thousand years of Christianity here on earth, Satan knows that, if Catholic Faith in the Holy Catholic Church disappears from earth, NO ONE will have the means of salvation. For with the disappearance of the pure Catholic Faith in the Catholic Church 'as handed down to us from the Apostles', the Catholic Church Herself would have vanished from this earth. For the Holy Council of Trent has declared as a Dogma of our Catholic Faith, that only Catholic Faith, that Supernatural, Infused and Divine Gift from God, whereby a mere mortal can believe all that the Holy Catholic Church proposes to us to believe, "is the beginning, the foundation, and the root of ALL justification". Only one thing can be "the beginning, the foundation, and the root of ALL justification", and Trent and Vatican I have made it crystal clear in the face of the Protestant Reformation, that this is only Catholic Faith in all its robust fullness, and not some effeminate 'generic christianity'.

This glorious Catholic Faith and the only Church which gives and nourishes it in Her Sacramental Life, are amply enriched by the founder of the Church and the Giver of Faith with all the human and supernatural resources to drive out evil. A good and holy bishop keeps evil at bay in his diocese and everybody, Catholics and non-Catholics alike, benefit from God's abundance in response. And so it goes down the line: good and holy parish priests keep evil at bay in their parishes, and holy Catholic parents keep evil removed not only from their children, but from their friends and neighbours who all benefit from God's largesse.

That is how it was meant that Salvation would not only invisibly grow globally as the Kingdom of God, but would also manifest itself in its beneficial, visible effects for all humanity wherever the Church was welcomed. Not without the Cross, as two thousand years of caring for the sheep can testify, but by stamping out evil. For it must always be borne in mind, that EVIL is not a thing in itself: evil is merely 'the absence of good', and the Catholic Church was meant by God to supply and restore the 'good' that 'evil' is lacking.

Bad bishops can invariably be recognized by the retreat of Good in their dioceses and by the flood of evil coming out of the woodwork to hamper the work of the true Catholic Faith. Thus if a Pope stresses that 'in the liturgy the Church salutes Mary of Nazareth as the Church's own beginning' and that 'Her fullness designates the beginning of the Church's journey', not only in Faith but in all the endless variety and capacity of Good the Church is capable of, then these words go a long way to explain why this Church has believed from times immemorial that knowledge of the true Catholic doctrine regarding the Blessed Virgin Mary will always be a key to the exact understanding of the Mystery of Christ, and of the Church's self-understanding of being the true Church founded by Christ. If in times of great religious upheavals the One, True Church needs to go back to "the beginning, the foundation, and the root" of Her self-understanding, then She will retreat to Her Marian roots in order to maintain and display Her true identity.

This explains how the Holy Spirit, always respecting the deepest wish of the Mother of God to be hidden, inspired the way to allow the Holy Church to acquire the fullest possible knowledge of Her Marian roots. At the time that the Early Church came to grips with the Mystery of Christ and of His Church, and the dignity of the role the Blessed Virgin Mary as the Mother of God and the 'New Eve' of the Redemption started to get hold of the instinct of Christendom, never to be relinquished, did the Wisdom Books of the Old Testament become for the Fathers of the early Church a rich source where this so desirable knowledge about the Blessed Virgin Mary in relation to the Catholic Church was to be found, readily expressed in words carefully selected under the inspiration of the Holy Spirit for that very purpose.

The personification of Wisdom as a singularly unique Lady, a Mother, a Bride, at times even introduced as speaking and acting as such, is so conducive to raising the meditating soul to the presence of the Blessed Virgin Mary, that such an identification could only come from the all-inspiring Mind of God. And if at times one feels compelled to transfer this rich information to an identification with the Church of which this exalted Lady has been made 'the fullness of the beginning', then such a natural application can again only be caused by the known Will of God, the Creator of these so precious pages and of their understanding in the Light of Faith.

We will commence with a passage from the Book of Proverbs, Ch. 8, wherein Wisdom briefly introduces Herself, declares with authority who will, and who will not, have access to Her, and then goes over to reveal Her origin.

> "I, Wisdom, dwell with experience, and possess good advice
>   and sound judgement.
> But, since they that fear the Lord must hate evil,
> All pride and boastfulness, the evil ways and the lying tongue I
>   hate.
> Mine are counsel and advice, mine are discernment and
>   strength.
> Through Me the rulers govern and are all the judges respected.

I love those who love Me, and those who wait early at My door
   shall gain access to Me.
With Me are riches and honour, enduring wealth and divine
   favour.
My fruit (1) is better than gold, yes, even the purest, Better than
   the finest silver My return.
I walk in the way of virtue, in the paths of justice,
Enriching those who love Me, filling their treasuries."

(1) JESUS. 'And blessed is the Fruit of Thy womb, Jesus.'

Right from the start, this passage marks the dividing line between 'those who have access to Me and those who will not'. These
words identify those for whom the Virgin Mary will remain a
closed secret, a 'sealed fountain', and what is necessary to gain access to Her hidden treasures and meanings. God knows we are all
sinners, but it is a peculiar type of sinner which has been singled
out here as being at war with Wisdom: the proud, the boasters,
those who out of habit persist with doing evil: those who 'walk evil
ways', and the liars. The many Catholics thus who know better
than the Church; those who boast about their own cleverness and
so persist in embracing as 'catholic' what is not, and worst of all,
those who misuse their position of authority, and who even stoop
to lying to present and enforce as 'catholic' what is evil and contrary to the Faith.

It is right here at the beginning, that Divine Authority declares
that 'in the ones such as these there will be found no Wisdom' and
(as will be made very clear) no love for the Mother of God.

It is also right here at the beginning, that Wisdom and the possession of it are identified with 'ruling'. This idea will never be abandoned. On the contrary, the sacred authors come back to this truth and develop it in a most forceful way. 'Through <u>Me</u> the rulers govern'. Christ is the King, the Ruler, the Centre of the Universe. It is only on Him, and on His Mystical Body in time, that the whole of creation and redemption are aligned. What is not aligned on Him or His Holy Church does not rule. It is as simple as that.

The decisive force on earth does not spring from technology, or from political power, armies, finance or economics. Ruling is the exclusive prerogative of Wisdom and Her children.

From observations such as these it must be considered more than a coincidence that the words spoken here by Wisdom call to mind the words uttered by the Blessed Virgin Mary in Her Magnificat. For Mary spoke these words after She had received 'the Blessed Fruit of Her womb', and in Her name Wisdom declares here that 'Her fruit is better than gold, even the purest'. We continue our quote from the book of Proverbs about Wisdom's origins:

"The Lord possessed Me in the beginning of His ways,
Before He made anything, from the beginning.
I was formed from eternity, and of old, before the earth was
    made.
The depths were not as yet and I was already conceived.
Neither had the fountains of waters as yet sprung out.
The mountains with their bulk had not as yet been established.
Before the hills I was brought forth.

He had not yet made the earth, nor the rivers, nor the poles of
     the world.
When He prepared the heavens I was there.
When with a certain law and compass He enclosed the depths;
When He established the sky above and poised the fountains of
     waters;
When He encompassed the sea with His bounds,
And set a law to the waters not to pass their limits;
When He balanced the foundations of the earth:
I WAS WITH HIM, forming all things, and was His delight
     every day,
Playing before Him at all times,
Playing on the surface of His earth,
Delighting to be with the sons of men."

In the pre-Vatican II Church, this extract from Wisdom's
origin was used as the first lesson of the Mass on the Feast of the
Immaculate Conception as a clear indication of the ancient saying
that, in the Catholic Church, the 'Lex Orandi' is the 'Lex Credendi':
the way the Church prays is the way She believes. Meaning, that the
Church does not think of the above quoted extract as referring exclusively to the Incarnate Son of God, but also to His Helpmate, the
'New Eve', bracketed with Him inseparably 'in the same Decree of
Predestination' as is clearly expressed here. The same extract is still
available in the new missal for Masses on feastdays of Our Lady.

'Sea', in prophetic language as being used here, is often an apt
description of 'restless humanity', humanity 'on the move', 'in
turmoil' or 'in revolt'. It is interesting to note that, according to the

belief of the Church in prayer, Our Lady's Immaculate Conception is, in the Divine Mind, the law by which the 'sea' is bounded and by which 'rising and restless waters are kept within their limits'. For those who are approaching the turbulent times of the reign of Antichrist and his global 'church' of darkness and revolt, this is a very consoling thought. And the sacred author concluded this extract with these words:

> Therefore, my children, listen to Me:
> Blessed are they that keep My ways.
> Hear instruction and be wise, and do not ignore it.
> Happy the man who obeys Me,
> Who watches daily at My gates, waiting at My doorposts.
> He who finds Me finds life, he shall have salvation from
>   His God.
> But he who misses Me, injures himself,
> And all who hate Me love death."....(2)

(2) First Lesson, Dec. 8, Feast of the Immaculate Conception in the old Roman Missal.

Here 'My ways' are placed in sharp contrast and in direct opposition to the 'evil ways I hate': the ways of pride, boastfulness and lying. The very ways by which RENEW, the 'Melbourne Guidelines for Religious (!) Education, and 'classroom sex education' are introduced, enforced and maintained, together with all those other programs that 'miss Her', and so cause death and injury to Catholics insane enough to use 'pastorals', the pulpit, 'catholic weeklies' seminars and 'imprimaturs' to spread the lies of Modernism in total defiance of what is written here with everlasting veracity:

"All who hate Me love death …"

said with as much conviction about Our Lady as it is said about Her unique Daughter, the Holy Catholic Church.

The remainder of the quotes will make it abundantly clear just what Wisdom understands by 'My ways'.

Over the next few days, from the second day to the fifth day inclusive, the quotes will be taken from selected passages out of the book of Wisdom, the central core of the Old Testament Wisdom literature. The quotes begin with ch. 6, v. 12 and go intermittently to ch. 9, v. 8.

The composition of the Book (it was first written in Greek) is much younger than the days of King Solomon, but that does not detract from its guaranteed inspired character nor from the fact that the unknown author must have made extensive use of written documentation which goes all the way back to King Solomon's days.

II

"Even to think about Her
shows understanding fully grown"

"Beautiful is Wisdom, Her brightness never grows dim.
She is readily seen by those who love Her;
And found by those who look for Her.
Quick to anticipate those who desire Her,
She makes Herself known to them.
Keep watch for Her at dawn and you will not be disappointed,
You will find Her sitting at your gate."

If the brightness of Our Blessed Lady 'never grows dim', but She is no longer 'readily seen' by the RENEWED and all their Modernist tutors and gurus, then the fault does not lie with Our Lady but with those Catholics who have driven Her away out of their contraceptive 'life styles' 'into the desert of oblivion', as St. John predicted in his Apocalypse (Ch. 12) would one day become a worldwide practise in human history in preparation for the 'Church of Darkness' of Antichrist. And what a 'church' that will be ...! A veritable 'synagogue of Satan' (Rev. 3: 9), in which Our Lord will never find the name of His Mother, the 'New Jerusalem', indelibly engraved on the pillars of its accursed 'sanctuary'.

'Keep watch for Her at dawn ...' Say the 6am Angelus with Her, preceded or followed if possible by a Holy Rosary, 'and you will find Her sitting at your gate', as the sacred author continues to explain in the next few lines:

> "Even to think about Her shows understanding fully grown;
> To be on the alert for Her will quickly allay your anxieties.
> He who keeps vigil for Her sake shall quickly be free from care."
> 'To be on the alert for Her will quickly allay your anxieties!'

If only the Priests who were anxious and uneasy about RENEW had remembered those indelible words! If they had been 'on the alert for Her', had studied the program to see if it had been written with Her in mind, as coming from Her Immaculate Heart, 'how quickly would they have been allayed about their anxieties' caused by their rejection of the program, after they had found out that RENEW has been written in an alien tongue, in a 'synagogue' in which the Name of the Blessed Virgin Mary does not appear on the pillars of its 'sanctuary'. A program that indeed invades the True Sanctuary of God to obliterate with its placards, posters and banners any remembrance of its Marian identity. If 'to think about her shows understanding fully grown', what then, one may well ask, does rejecting Her reveal ...!

How could Catholics ever miss Her brightness unless She was driven out of their lives? For the sacred author goes on inexorably:

> "She walks about looking for those who are worthy of Her,
> And graciously shows Herself to them on the road,
> In every thought of theirs coming to meet them."

'In every thought …' Constantly busy with those who love Her, Mary encourages them at every moment 'to be on the alert for Her' so they would have 'understanding fully grown', which in final analysis can only come about by the fusion of our lives with the Divine Life of God: the ultimate aim of Salvation. If these are the lasting effects of a great and constant devotion to Our Blessed Lady, then who on earth, in direct contradiction to the inspiring Spirit of God, can maintain that Our Lady is an obstacle to love of God! And that hellish programs like RENEW must now take Her place in the understanding that they will do a better job than She. When it is written that 'those who miss Me, injure themselves …'

And this is only the beginning of God's revelations about His Bride and His Mother, composed in such a marvellous way that they form one organic unity with His revelation in the New Testament, where all this could remain hidden 'out of respect for the deepest inclination of the Blessed Virgin Mary', as it had already been revealed with such great tact and precision in the Old Testament.

"Of Her, the most sure beginning is the desire for discipline."

Here, without any shadow of doubt, the Holy Spirit has singled out for all generations what, in final analysis, must be considered to be THE most serious obstacle to a lasting devotion to the Mother of God. Here is being chartered the 'submerged rock' on which Judas' and all other half-hearted attempts at intimacy with God flounder. Here is being pointed out why and how bishops and priests, nuns, brothers and laity who embraced or enforced Modernism in its endless and virulent varieties, failed the final test: 'NO DISCIPLINE'

Tolerate in your life 'No Discipline of the mind' declares Pope St. Pius X in 1910, unveiling the hallmark of the 'one-world church of darkness', then your life will also be in the grip of 'No curb on the Passions', i.e. no discipline of morals, held up by the same Holy Father as the other hallmark of the 'church of darkness'. (Our Apostolic Mandate, 1910.) And with that papal reminder of the Divine teaching quoted the Saint has reinforced for our times how 'the most sure beginning of all intimacy with Wisdom' evaporates.

The 'sure beginning' of a lasting love for the Mother of God disintegrates if the divine harmony between 'natural understanding' (truth ascertainable by reason) and 'supernatural insights' (Faith in all Revealed Truth) is deliberately scuttled on the submerged rock of no discipline in thinking. When any thought, or any 'faith' is considered as viable and acceptable as any other.

The 'discipline of the mind' is destroyed as long as 'the impossibility of contrary 'truths' existing side by side' (Pope John XIII) is denied, and instead contradiction is hailed as another foundation of one's life through the willful embrace of spurious programs and philosophies.

If, what is quite common nowadays amongst many priests and religious that defiance and dissent from Church teaching and the open contradiction of the Faith, are to be considered the same and 'just as Catholic' as St. Paul's demand for "obedience to the Faith" (Rom. 1:15), then no corrupted thinking as the result of such dissolution in mind and morals will ever 'chime in with divine Revelation'. Pope Pius XII has laid down forever that this chiming in with Revelation only takes place 'as by a pre-established harmony' between Revelation and the pure mind open to the discipline of clear thinking, of which the Everlasting Philosophy of St. Thomas Aquinas is both the ultimate in training and achievement. And 'not chiming in with Revelation' is, of course, akin to "the second death" in St. John's writings.

Why? Because the 'discipline of the mind', the ascertainment of all Truth, is the necessary prerequisite for the indispensible 'curb on the passions', singled out here as 'the most sure beginning of Her' who is introduced to us in all Her imposing majesty as being the personification of Wisdom.

"Of Her, the most sure beginning is the desire for discipline.
Care for discipline means loving Her;
Loving Her means keeping Her laws;
Obeying Her laws guarantees incorruptibility,
and incorruptibility leads to the presence of God.
And thus the desire for Wisdom leads to Sovereignty.
If then you find pleasure in throne and sceptre, you princes of
    peoples,
Honour Wisdom, that you may reign forever."

Who but the Holy Spirit could be expected to compress so succinctly, in a mere five lines, a whole life of Marian spirituality: from the cradle to the grave and beyond, right into 'the presence of God'?

If ever anyone needed convincing that love for Our Lady 'leads to the presence of God', then the proof of it is found right here, guaranteed by God under divine inspiration. We must leave the unfolding of the unbelievable riches of the three lines in the middle of this quote:

> "Care for discipline means loving Her;
> Loving Her means keeping Her laws;
> Obeying Her laws guarantees incorruptibility,"

being the program of a lifetime, to the next chapter, where they will be discussed in conjunction with further revelations by the Holy Spirit of the incomparable majesty of Wisdom. Here we can only introduce the quote as a whole in honour of Our Blessed Lady.

And what sort of life can the fortunate finder of this rare and magnificent pearl of Marian piety expect?

'A life of Sovereignty'!

A life of being 'in charge'; of being 'a ruler'. Once again it is stated here plainly in so many words: 'And thus the desire for Wisdom leads to Sovereignty'. To reinforce this whole idea once and for all, the sacred author, with the Authority of God, enlarges on his subject. 'If then you find pleasure in throne and sceptre, you princes of people', if you want to be 'in charge', if you like to rule for the benefit of all, even if stretched out on a bed of pain in a hospital, or subjected to the direst and most abject poverty: "HONOUR WISDOM, that you may reign forever ...."

For the benefit of the greatest possible understanding of what has been said here, it may be necessary to run ahead on our narrative and to lift the veil on something that is still to come. Sometimes it is necessary to teach 'by contrast', and for that reason the sentence that is going to be quoted now is all-decisive!

"Only to the fool is She unbearable,

The <u>undisciplined</u> man does not stay with Her for long:

She will weigh on him like a heavy stone,

And he will lose no time in throwing Her off."

Yes, of Her the most sure beginning is the desire for discipline!

III

"For She is to men an inexhaustible treasure"

Toward the end of Day I in this narrative it was stated that the remainder of the quotations from the Wisdom Books will make it abundantly clear just what Wisdom, the Holy Virgin, understands by 'My Ways'. In order that maximum benefit can be derived from what is still to come, the 'discipline of the mind' requests that a good understanding is acquired of what went before, and that we have a closer look at the revelations the Holy Spirit has summarized for us so succinctly in those mere five lines in the passage of Sacred Scripture quoted in the previous day of this novena. Each line is filled with experiences enough to fill a lifetime; all of these are controlled and permeated with that sole beginning of Her: the 'desire for discipline', and all are geared to the one final end: 'to come into the presence of God'.

Let us lift the eyes of our prayerful mind for a brief moment towards a Virgin in Nazareth, about to be visited by the Archangel Gabriel. Even of Her it must be said that only after the need for all the foregoing had been firmly accepted by the one, God had enclosed from all eternity as the 'Woman of Genesis' in the same Decree of Predestination as the Son of God, could God ask Her, as His Bride, for Her consent in bringing about the Incarnation of His Son. Only the purest 'natural understanding' of the clearest possible thinking could be expected 'to chime in', and fuse, with the 'supernatural insights' demanded by Faith, needed for the fullness of

Divine Revelation about to be made at this most momentous moment in history. If 'the desire for discipline' is for anyone 'the most sure beginning of Her', then this can only be so because it was also <u>Her own</u> most sure beginning, the beginning of 'Her ways' as our own Mother, in order that She too would have the most perfect harmony between natural understanding and supernatural insights at the very moment that God would require the perfection of this discipline of the mind to be present most on earth ...

For it is only on the basis of that 'pre-established harmony' between <u>all</u> truths, natural as well as supernatural, that God can allow the fullest understanding of His Divine Mysteries to be granted to a mind, which has disciplined itself by the habit of the clearest possible thinking, to avoid jarring the perfect harmony. And 'at the beginning of Her ways' Our Blessed Mother must have possessed that vital discipline to the highest degree in a mere human being, if in the Mind of the Holy Spirit She was to be declared blessed by all generations (Magnificat). If up to then no greater, allround perfection had been found on our poor earth, then in Mary, we are in the presence of the Old Testament 'created wisdom', by means of which the Divine and human could fuse to bring about the Incarnation.

If clear thinking in ordinary human affairs is necessary for us all, so we do not fall into deceit, and do not let ourselves be guided by error, then this natural understanding becomes even more imperative for those to whom the eternal salvation of Christ's flock has been entrusted. In bishops and priests, in teachers and parents, not only deceitful thinking, but even the habit of sloppy, shallow and erroneous thinking is incompatible with the so necessary 'chiming in with Revelation', if souls have to be brought into the presence of God along 'My Ways'. And if the destiny of nations and peoples has been entrusted to the 'Wisdom the leads to Sovereignty', then the utmost care in the discipline of the mind and the curbing of the passions 'is the most sure beginning' of that reign.

Finally, in Her liturgy the Holy Catholic Church has claimed the Virgin Mary to be Her own beginning, and has identified Her with the 'Wisdom' of the Old Testament. From this it follows that only a Marian Church, a Church in whose Sanctuary the pillars are engraved with the name of Her who at the Incarnation became the 'New Jerusalem', can rightly be considered to be the exclusive continuation of what the Virgin Mary began. For it is necessary that this Church is first 'Marian' before it can be truly 'Petrine'! As promised in the Introduction, this 'one-liner' too can be traced to the mind of the Church, expressing in its brevity the gist of the Christmas message the Holy Father John Paul II delivered to the assembled Curia in 1987. Although the Petrine aspect of the Church is essential, the Holy Father said, its Marian profile is both anterior in time and superior in nature, as in the Blessed Virgin Mary the Holy Church sees at once Her own beginning as well as Her own fullness.

So now things start to fall into place.

Of 'Wisdom', the Holy Spirit has clearly indicated to all of us both 'the beginning of Her ways': the desire for discipline, as well as 'the ultimate end': being led into the presence of God. From now on any Catholic reading this in the New Dispensation, joins any Jew reading this in the Old one in being fully preoccupied with what Divine Inspiration has so succinctly placed <u>in between</u> these two extremes:

'care for discipline ...'
'loving Her ...'
'obeying Her laws ...'

And in the fullness of Revelation in the New Testament, we discern that this spot in the middle is now the exclusive reserve of only <u>one</u> Church, the one which is required to be 'Marian' in order to be fully 'Petrine'. For the same Holy Father who has redirected our attention to this age-old truth, had written earlier in the same year in his Marian encyclical *Redemptorist Mater*:

"Mary embraces each and everyone <u>in</u> the Church,
and each and everyone <u>through</u> the Church."

This can only mean one thing. The same 'slot' that had once been reserved for the ways to reach wisdom in the Old Testament (and by which Wisdom Herself had come "into the presence of God" at the threshold of the New Testament), i.e. the road of those three important lines on the middle:

'care for discipline ...'
'loving Her ...'
'obeying Her laws ...'

has even in the fullness of Time remained the exclusive reserve for Wisdom, but now transferred to Her Marian Church, 'in which and through which' (according to the words of the Holy Father) the fulfillment of Wisdom, Our Blessed Lady, once again beckons each and everyone to the fullness of Revelation and Redemption. Still with the same beginning: 'the desire for discipline'; and with the same end in view: 'to come into the presence of God'; and still with the same three ways in the middle:

'Care for discipline in mind and heart means loving the Church.'
'Loving Her means keeping Her Laws.'
'Obeying Her law of Faith (Rom. 1:5) guarantees incorruptibility.'

No compromise!

We have divine confirmation that this total identification between Mother and Daughter is part of the 'pre-established harmony' of which Pope Pius XII wrote in 1950 (Humani Generis)

In the twelfth chapter of the Book of Revelation 'the Woman chased into the desert' is but One dramatic representation of what is happening to TWO indistinguishable Realities at the time: to the Catholic Church, and to any love, thought and devotion for the Blessed Virgin Mary here on earth during the chaos of the final preparation before the appearance of the 'First Beast', and of the establishment of the 'One-World 'religion' of the Second Beast'. So too ever since the Wisdom Books came forth from the inspiring Mind of God as the product of His faithful instruments, Wisdom saw beyond the Old Testament prefiguration of the 'New Eve' of the New Testament, to a future Church created in Her sacred image and likeness, fully equipped to carry on and complete Mary's sacred commission 'until the end of time'.

So, what did the man, to whom God had once said "I will give you a heart wise and shrewd as none before you has had and none will have after you", supposedly do, after he reputedly wrote down the immortal words 'about the sure beginning and end of Wisdom' we have just studied? What did he do? He prayed …

> "And so I (Solomon) prayed, and understanding was given to
>   me.
> I entreated, and the Spirit of Wisdom came to me.
> I esteemed Her more than sceptres and thrones,
> Compared with Her I held riches as nothing.
> I reckoned no priceless stone to be Her peer.
> For compared with Her all gold is as dust,
> And beside Her silver ranks as mud.
> More than health and beauty did I love Her,
> Preferred Her to the light,
> since Her radiance never dims.
> In Her company greater good came my way,
> Because immeasurable riches lie in Her hands.
> I enjoyed all this since Wisdom brought it with Her,
> And without knowing as yet that She was their Mother.
> In sincerity I learned to know Her,
> And without envy I pass Her on.
> For She is to men an inexhaustible treasure

And those who acquire it gain God's friendship
As they become pleasing to Him by the gifts of Her virtue.
Hidden or visible, I have come to the knowledge of everything,
Instructed by Wisdom who designed it all."

Wish that Our Lady was loved like that by every Catholic! But since the Holy Church which must be fully 'Marian' before She can be 'Petrine' is no longer loved by millions of Her children, and has been chased into the wilderness by those who deserted Her, to make room for the harlot 'church' of RENEW and kindred weeds, so also the Holy Woman, in whose sacred image the True Bride of the Lamb of God had been conceived, has been deserted as well, and Her memory has been chased into the same desert of oblivion. And the banners of the NEW revolution, of defiance and apostasy, are brought into the House of God, obscuring Her sacred name, 'indelibly engraved by Her Son on the pillars of the only Sanctuary He loves'. But has it not been written with the same indelible force:

> "Thou shalt not bring into the House of God the wages of a prostitute." (Deut. 23: 18).

And also:

> "Come here, and I will show you the punishment given to the notorious harlot ..." (Rev. 17: 1).

What Wisdom deserved and granted in the Old Testament, Our Lady and the Holy Catholic Church deserve and will grant in the New Testament. Why?

"For within Her is a Spirit intelligent, holy,
Unique, manifold, subtle,
Active, incisive, unsullied,
Lucid, invulnerable, benevolent, sharp,
Irresistible, beneficent, loving to man,
Steadfast, dependable, unperturbed,
All-powerful, all-surveying, penetrating all other spirits,
No matter how intelligent, pure and most subtle they might be.
For Wisdom is quicker than anything that moves;
She pervades and permeates all things through the power of
    Her purity."

For two thousand years the Holy Catholic Church has believed that this writing was inspired by God having Our Blessed Lady in Mind, as well as the Holy Church that would one day be conceived in Her spotless image and likeness.

And now for the big question: Can the same quote be applied to the 'church' envisaged by RENEW or any other 'New Age' drivel? To the 'church' forseen by Pope St. Pius X, the One-World 'Church of Darkness', that modern day agglomerate with 'no discipline of the mind nor curb on the passions'? Which is no church at all, but only resembles the 'Synagogue of Satan' in loathsomeness and insanity? Obviously not! And so these 'spirits' and 'churches' are doomed; for, like Wisdom, 'the Virgin is quicker than anything that moves ...'

And because of that, because She is there 'before anyone or anything else', and because 'She pervades and permeates all things through the power of Her Purity', everything is forced to take its measure from Her, must declare its worth before Her, must prove that it comes from Her Marian Church, from Her Marian profile, even before any claim to a 'Petrine' aspect can be scrutinized! For that is what is meant by that 'Everlasting Enmity' established by God in Paradise.

If it is fully realised what is being stated here, that the Holy Catholic Church has a right and a duty to ask of everything: 'How Marian is it'?, then before RENEW can claim to come 'from the Church', that is, can claim that it is 'Petrine', it first has to show that it is Marian! That is, show that it has 'within itself a Spirit, intelligent, holy, unique ...' That 'its most sure beginning is a desire for discipline'! That 'its care for discipline shows its love for the Mother of God and the Marian Church'. That 'this love is reflected in keeping Her laws'! And that 'its obedience to Church's Law of Faith guarantees incorruptibility, leading to the presence of God'!

Furthermore, it must show that, with Our Blessed Lady, 'it pervades and permeates all things through the power of its PURITY'!

Finally, programs like RENEW which claim to come 'from the Mind of the Church', i.e. lay claim to being 'Petrine', must satisfy the Church 'that they possess the knowledge of the true Catholic doctrine regarding the Blessed Virgin Mary', in order that they too may be a 'key to the exact understanding of the Mystery of Christ and of the Church'.

All this, as we all know, is an impossible request to demand from a harlot.

Here, we must admit, the 'Church Militant' as well as the 'Ecclesia Docens' or Magisterium, have been given by Eternal Wisdom a most incisive weapon in our war with the 'forces of Darkness', totally consistent with what created Wisdom had put so concisely previously as 'the beginning of HIS ways'. In Genesis, God put 'the Everlasting Enmity' not between Himself and Satan but between 'thee and the Woman, and between thy seed and Hers'! Whoever can prove to have 'the Woman of Genesis, 'Wisdom' Our Lady, and the Holy Church created in Her image and likeness on side, is fighting on the side of <u>God</u>. All those who are opposed to this are 'thy seed'! And the mortal combat is about what lives in between. The Unity of the Triune God is reflected in the consistency of Sacred Scripture. The enmity is still between Our Lady and Lucifer, and is still as relentless a war as it was on that first day when it became established many thousands of years ago, no matter what the RENEWED and their Modernist gurus may think themselves or may try to tell us.

IV

"She is the reflection of the Eternal Light"

We began our investigations into the origins of Wisdom – the First Day - with a most majestic declaration, made by no one on behalf of Wisdom but by Wisdom Herself:

"The Lord possessed Me in the beginning of His Ways ..."

No doubt not a few readers may have gone back to this part of the narrative, drawn by the majesty of those indelible words, if not to the actual text, then at least in the solitude of their meditating minds.

"Before He made anything, from the beginning. I was formed from eternity, and of old, before the earth was made."

And so Wisdom reveals how, with His Incarnate Son and His virginal Mother steadfast in His Mind, the Creator sprinkled, with lavish hand, the traces of His treasures (still only enclosed "within the confines of the same Decree of Predestination") through the length and breadth of His Creation.

And just as in any performance of world class, the heroine is allowed to appear and speak on Her own, and on Her own behalf, if only to make the spell bound audience long even more intensely to witness the final reunion, so too here in the 'Divina Comedia':

"The depths were not as yet and I was already conceived."

'Depths' are measured against Me! When He prepared the Heavens, I was there. And when He balanced the foundations of the earth, He had Me in mind, as one day His Divine Son would do when balancing the foundations of His Church.

As with all God's handiwork, the meaning is disarmingly simple, yet at the same time totally inexhaustible.

No one but a fool leaves a great performance after only the introduction of the players and the outline of the plot, in preference for a rowdy orgy with his dissolute mates, as at present the Modernists are doing. A great audience stays, wishing to be swept away towards the inevitable climax, and beyond, by the unifying force of the end. And now a great climax is at hand. The Woman has been chased into the desert. Her cry of defiance: "Before you can claim to do this in the name of Peter, you must make it credible that you are doing this in My name as your depths of depravity too are measured against Me", thrown in the face of Her Catholic pursuers, has enraged "the seed of the serpent". And now the divine Playwright will attend to His duty, bound to reveal who it is, who is being so remorselessly banished from the company of the 'civilised world'. Who are the villains-in-pursuit, trying desperately "to look like the Lamb, but who speak and act more like the Dragon". (Rev. 13: 11)

> "For She is a breath of the Majesty of God,
> Pure emanation of the Glory of the Almighty,
> Hence nothing impure can touch Her.
> She is the reflection of the Eternal Light,
> Untarnished mirror of God's active power,
> The image of His perfection.
> Although alone, She can do all;

Herself unchanging, She makes all things new.

In each generation She enters into holy souls,

Forming them into friends of God and prophets.

For God loves only those who live with Wisdom.

She is indeed more splendid than the sun,

She outshines all the constellations.

Compared with light She takes precedence.

For light must yield to night,

But over Wisdom evil will never triumph.

She deploys Her strength from one end of the earth to the other,

It is She who orders all things for good."

What can we say? Where does one start? Do we begin with the Holy Spirit Who, because of Our Lady's desire to remain hidden, could not divulge in the New Testament in such exquisite detail what is being revealed here in the Old Testament about the splendour and glory of the Immaculate Conception? Shall we begin with Our Lady herself? Or rather with Her Daughter, the Holy Catholic Church, conceived and created in Her own spotless image and likeness? Perhaps it is safer to start with the latter and 'work our way up'.

Yes, we feel we are here in the presence of the Bride of the Lamb of God, as She came forth from the pierced Heart of Our Redeemer, washed clean and spotless in the water and Blood that flowed from His side while He was still nailed to His Cross - truly the 'New Creation.'

Is it not true that, after Our Lord's Ascension into Heaven, this Church does appear to be alone in a hostile and frivolous world? 'Although alone, She can do all. Herself unchanging, She makes all things new'. "A glorious Church having no spot or wrinkle" (Eph. 5: 27), enjoying Her perfect and perennial youth. (Pope John XIII).

Yes, only to the Holy Catholic Church of God depicted here has it been given 'to deploy Her strength from one end of the earth to the other, as it is She alone who, before the second coming of Christ, has been given His authority to order all things for good'. Unfailingly then 'in each generation', as stated here, 'this Church enters into holy souls, forming them into friends of God and prophets'; for truly, 'God loves those who live with Wisdom'. That is, all those of each and all generations who are not antagonistic to 'Her Ways' and who 'desire discipline' in order that they may find 'the beginning of Her'.

And if already so much of what the Holy Spirit reveals here can be said about the Daughter, then what about the Mother of this magnificent creation? Maybe, as St. Paul says, human words will finally fail and come to an end, but God will go on unfolding His treasures locked up in this 'sealed fountain' in the middle of this hidden Paradise.

Where could anyone expect to find a more apt description of the Immaculate Conception? Where else could one hope to be given a more majestic beginning of the Blessed Virgin Mary: "She is the reflection of the Eternal Light, untarnished mirror of God's active power, the image of His perfection", only to be matched by the glorious finale: "but over Wisdom evil will never triumph;" and what about all the revelations in between?

No wonder the Holy Catholic Church is at Her most beautiful when She is close to Her Marian roots; for it is here that we find scriptural confirmation of the weighty words of Pope John Paul II:

"Knowledge of the true Catholic doctrine regarding the Blessed Virgin Mary will always be a key to the exact understanding of the Mystery of Christ and of the Church." (RM. #47)

Yes here we are in the presence of a creature, a Virgin, a Mother, a Bride, a Queen, whom it is impossible to veil any longer by the description of 'Wisdom'. This creature is unique, and can only be a person of the most pure royal blood. She is destined for great things, to scale great heights and to know great sorrow, for – as is written of Her in the continuation of this magnificent saga – "the Lord of all has loved Her". And God has known sorrow.

Whose Daughter is this royal Maiden? The Daughter of God the Father. Whose Bride will She be? The Bride of God the Holy Spirit. And then, the last one of the burning questions in the minds of all the angels: of whom will She be the Mother? She is destined to be the Mother of the Son of God, the Mother of God. And with that, the Mother of all God's children ... no wonder, then, that the Holy Spirit allows His human scribe to continue to write for all generations:

"She it was I loved and searched for from my youth.
I resolved to have Her as my Bride,
For I fell in love with Her beauty.
She glories in Her noble birth,
For She lives in communion with God,
And the Lord of all has loved Her.

Yes, She is an initiate in the mysteries of God's knowledge,
Making choice of the works He is to do."
"Making choice of the works He is to do ..."

How could anyone but the inspiring God ever have had an ink-ling at this stage of the revelations, how literally true this would be one day, when the Son of God would be Mary's child in Nazareth ...

And then, in one unbelievable sweep, in one breathtaking pan-orama over human events, the Holy Spirit gets hold of all man's endeavours, and details, with divine accuracy and supreme author-ity, just how complete is Wisdom's mastery over world history; how far extends the realm of the Catholic Church; how penetrating is the reign of the Immaculate Heart; how absolute the Kingdom of God!

A. "If in this life <u>wealth</u> is a desirable possession,
    What is more wealthy than Wisdom whose work
      is everywhere?"
B. "Or if it is <u>intellect</u> that is to be pursued,
    Who in the whole world is a better craftsman than
      She?"
C. "Or if it be <u>virtue</u> you love,
    All Her actions are directed to this end,
    Since it is She who teaches temperance and prudence,
      Justice and fortitude,
    And nothing in life is more useful to men than these."
D. "Or if you are eager for <u>wide experience</u>,

She knows the past and forecasts the future;

She knows the meaning of maxims and the solution of riddles.

Signs and wonders She knows beforehand together with the vicissitudes of ages and times."

* Pursuing <u>wealth</u> without first consulting Wisdom;
* pursuing <u>intellect</u> without the 'discipline of the mind': that only 'sure beginning of Her' on anyone's road to what Trent and Vatican I have defined as "the beginning, root and foundation of ALL justification: Catholic Faith";
* even engaging in a life of <u>virtue</u> without the possession of the cardinal virtues, revealed here as being intimately joined to Her;
* in fact hankering after <u>any</u> human <u>experience</u> without the firm guidance of "Her who is an initiate in the mysteries of God's knowledge"

is a sheer waste of time, to which the terrible mess in which not only our present world, but so many Catholic lives find themselves, can testify! "She knows the past … etc." How forcefully are we reminded here of Our Lady of Fatima, and how the Holy Catholic Church shares in this prophetic mission of Her Mother and Model!

Yes, our world s in a terrible mess, and our heavenly Mother came down from heaven to warn us. Yet, even after this "great sign appeared in heaven" (Rev. 12 :1), St. John tells us "the people of the earth would not repent and praise Him". (Rev. 16: 9,11)

But they will still have no excuse, for long before this universal rejection towards the end of time was recorded in Sacred Scripture, did the Holy Spirit reveal what <u>should</u> have happened:

"So I resolved to take Her to share my life ..."
If only because of what follows in the next few lines

- the infallible reward for any sincere effort to put into practise all that has been set out before;
- this crown on the grand finale of the greatest show on earth;
- this complete 'chiming in with Divine Revelation of the human with the Divine,

if only all of this, the union of the Catholic Church with the Mother of God under the God-willed veil of Wisdom had been accepted and had become the core and centre of every RCIA program since Vatican II, what a flood of love for the Catholic Church and for the Blessed Virgin Mary would have been unleashed over our drought stricken earth! How, as in the vision of Isaiah, 'the desert would have bloomed' (Is. 35: 1), the desert into which 'the Woman has now been banished' (Rev. 12: 14) by those Catholics who did not want to repent and 'make room for Her in their homes' (Jo. 19: 27).

"So I resolved to take Her to share my life,
knowing She would be my counsellor in prosperity,
My comfort in cares and sorrow.
Through Her I shall be acclaimed where people gather,

And honoured among elders, although still a youth.

I shall be considered shrewd when I sit in judgement,

in the presence of the great I shall be admired.

They will wait on my silence and pay attention when I speak.

Even if I speak at some length, they will lay their hands on their lips.

By means of Her, immortality shall be mine.

And I shall leave an everlasting memory to my successors.

I shall govern peoples, and nations will be subject to me.

At the sound of my name fearsome despots will be afraid.

I shall show myself kind to my people and valiant in battle.

When I return home I shall take my ease with Her, for nothing is bitter in Her company,

To share with Her does not cause pain but only gladness and joy."

If the intensity of this God-inspired crescendo is the guaranteed fate of every Marian Saint, then it is also, to a very large extent, the fate of every Marian Catholic who has managed in his or her short life to combine a great love for the Mother of God with a great love for the Catholic Church and for the glory of the Catholic Faith within Her.

Again, what can we say? Where can we start? How can we add to the abundance and generosity of this Divine Revelation? What can a mere human do to add to the power of this global control? How utterly true it is, that RULING is the absolute prerogative of Wisdom and Her children!

"By means of Her, immortality shall be mine ..."

Try to tell that to the latest pop-group! See how open our case hardened Modernists are to this, entrenched as they are in their 'catholic education offices', from where all the corruption of the Catholic Faith in Catholic schools emanates. Try to get this accepted by those in the Catholic clergy who in their relentless push for 'married priests', 'women priests', 'local church', 'small groups', have become adamant that here, in their 'new catholicism', permanency and 'everlastingness' have finally been found!

Vain hope! Scripture remains adamant: immortality was NEVER the coveted crown granted to the popularity contest enjoyed by those "who leave My people in their sins" and who wander over roads far removed from 'Her Ways' in order to achieve this. "Brood of vipers! Who warned you to fly from the retribution that is coming? .... Even now, the axe is laid to the roots of the trees, so that any tree which fails to produce good fruit will be cut down and thrown on the fire" (Mt. 3: 9-10), hardly an advertisement for immortality, or even permanency!

"At the sound of my name fearsome despots will be afraid."

The greatest fear directing the iron fist of Modernism is a public confrontation with immortal and everlasting Truth. Thus the Number One concern of its diabolical adherents is to avoid a showdown at all cost. And ever since the take-over of all Catholic outlets by this modern strain of despots at the close of Vatican II, intrepid Catholics on the side of Truth have had ample opportunity to testify to the accuracy of the above quoted words: "At the sound of my name fearsome despots will be afraid," whenever they flood the "dark workshops" of Modernism with "the reflection of the Eternal Light". For "beautiful is Wisdom, Her brilliance never grows dim". And it does not matter if the Eternal Light of Church teaching is held up by a housewife, a theologian or a Pope: the fear it inspires is always the same!

"I shall govern peoples, and nations will be subject to me."

From Light to Power ...

This is not only Wisdom speaking here: Our Blessed Lady or the Holy Catholic Church, but the children and servants of Wisdom! And the truth of the statement loses nothing of its impact even if, only ONE child, ONE servant of Wisdom is speaking! And if what is being expressed here, is true of the children and servants, even for only ONE, how ever more true will it be for their Mother and Queen, in whose name these servants, this one child, will rule ...

Over the last twenty years we have witnessed the power for evil a bishop has, a parish priest, a theologian, a teacher, a nun. Yet they cannot impose a perversion of the Truth in the name of the Catholic Church, but only in their own evil names, and only over those who hail them, those 'whose sure beginning was not the desire for discipline'. For all of these it has been written: "All pride and boastfulness, the evil ways, the lying tongue I hate!" And so there is a superior force 'to which they too will be subject', even if only wielded by a solitary child of Wisdom in the possession of the power of the Catholic Faith: "the beginning, root and foundation of ALL justification". (Trent, Vatican I). In the face of the apparent global control of the forces of Antichrist, this vastly superior 'power-to-rule' of the children of wisdom, of even ONE of Her children, cannot be stressed enough. If it is doubted in any way, that child will sink, like Peter did, instead of rule!

"When I return home ..."

"When I return home, after proving myself 'valiant in battle' in the service of Wisdom, I shall take my ease with Her ..."

What a home-coming that must be ...!

V

"... and protect me with Her glory"

"Thinking thus within myself, reflecting it all in my heart,

- That immortality is found in kinship with Wisdom,
- Pure contentment in Her friendship,
- Inexhaustible riches in the works of Her hands,
- Intelligence in the intimate conversations with Her,
- And renown in the participation of Her discourse:

I went in all directions seeking by what means I might make Her mine."

The great height has been scaled. From the breathtaking view he now commands, the holy author is fully aware that he has reached the top, and that, as far as he knows, nothing that he should have said or done has been left out. Now, before the next mystery can be unfolded and the next move can be made, linking the past with what is still to come, he lingers, and in the prayers of his mind and heart he takes stock of all that has been achieved so far, so that this organic unity between past and future can be properly taken care of. And what a recapitulation it is! In brevity and magnificence and glories of the final union with Wisdom on those lofty heights, match line for line the five line invitation of Her beginning, expressed in 'The Second Day'.

'Immortality', 'Pure contentment', 'inexhaustible riches', 'Intelligence', 'Renown': nothing has been left out, nothing has been over-looked. Whatever the human heart can desire, it is all there as already promised it would be in the unfolding of the panorama during the ascent of Mount Carmel on 'The Fourth Day', and as already contained so succinctly within those five lines of Wisdom's initial invitation.

Where else but in language guaranteed and inspired by the Holy Spirit would we ever hope to find what it means to be a child of Mary, to be a member of the Holy Catholic Church? Reading and re-reading the above in conjunction with what has been revealed about the beginning of Wisdom, and about the universal grasp She has over all creation, how on earth is it possible that we can point to <u>any</u> person who could maintain in all seriousness 'that devotion to Our Blessed Lady is an obstacle to God, or that the Holy Catholic Church must be bypassed for the obtainment of perfect union with Christ', if according to the Revelation made here, whatever is needed for that perfect union with God and Christ, is only found here 'in kinship with Wisdom'? That is, is only found contained within the one person in whom God became Man, and in the one Church He created in Her spotless image and likeness, to continue the fruits of the Incarnation?

If the totality of God was enclosed within Mary's womb as a result of Her consent, and with it the totality of the Redemption, and if 'in the liturgy the Church salutes Mary of Nazareth as the Church's own beginning', then the reign of Mary must extend as far as the reign of Her Son, and the influence of His Body the

Church must by necessity extend as far as the influence of both Her Head and Her Mother.

If immortality is the final union with God in eternity, away from 'the Second Death' (Rev. 2: 1; 20: 6), and if the Holy Spirit guarantees here with absolute veracity 'that immortality is found in kinship with Wisdom', and that 'God loves those who live with Wisdom', then divine continuity demands that, what is being inspired here with eternal veracity in the Old Testament, receives all its glory, meaning and fulfillment from the New, without any harm to this divine continuity and veracity nor to the thrust of the original revelation in the Old. And the only revelation in the New Testament that can lay claim to this veracity in the Old is the Redemption by the Son of God at the heart of which we find the consent of 'the Woman of Genesis', 'the New Eve', 'the Church's own beginning', 'Mary of Nazareth', who alone can lay Her royal claim to be the personification and fulfillment of what God revealed in the Old Testament about 'Wisdom': His future Bride, Mother and Queen. And with that only one other creation has the legal right to do the same after having inherited this royal claim: the Church and Daughter of which this Bride, Mother and Queen would be the beginning!

And because every part of the Divina Comedia is crying out for a Man for this Woman, a Son for this Mother, a King for this Queen, a Mother for this Daughter and a Head for this Church, that still in no way does diminish the overriding importance that it is by a Divine Decree that the New Adam 'should also not be alone', but should have His own New Eve; that the King is searching for a Queen, the Son for a Mother; that the Mother must have a

Daughter, and that the Head should not be without a Body, the Church. And can any law be invoked against God's freedom to reveal any of this already in the Old Testament, in the most exquisite detail He likes, in preparation of His future plans in the New?

Now, from the dazzling heights reached here and enthralled by the visions provided with such promise, is it any wonder that the Old starts praying for the New, imploring God to hasten that blessed day containing the fullness of revelation, since what He revealed in the Old has already such a share in His eternal beauty?

And with this, the Old Testament begins in the most literal sense "to call for Mary":

> "But I understood that I could not otherwise possess Her but
>   by the gift of God."
>   - A mark itself of understanding, to know Whose posses-
>   sion She is –
> "I turned to the Lord in prayer,
> And entreated Him, praying with all my heart:
> 'God of our ancestors, Lord of mercy,
> 'Who by Your Word have made all things,
> 'And in Your Wisdom have fitted man,
> 'To rule the creatures that come from You,
> 'To govern the world in holiness and justice,
> 'To wield authority in honesty of soul:
> 'GRANT ME WISDOM, Consort of Your throne,
> 'And do not reject me from the number of your children.
> 'For I am Your servant, the son of Your handmaid,

'A feeble man, only short-lived, with little understanding
     of justice and the laws.

'Even if one was perfect among the sons of men:

'If he lacked the Wisdom that comes from You,

'He would still count for nothing.

'But with You is Wisdom, She knows Your works,

'She who was present when You made the world.

'She understands what is pleasing in Your eyes,

'And what agrees with Your commandments.

'SEND HER FORTH from the holy heavens,

'Despatch Her speedily from Your throne of glory,

'That She may be with me, and work with me,

'And teach me what is pleasing to You,

'Since She knows and understands everything.

'She will guide me prudently in my undertakings,

'And protect me with Her glory.

'Only then will all I do be acceptable,

'Shall I govern Your people justly,

'And shall I be worthy of my father's throne.

'What man indeed can know the intentions of God?

'Or can divine His Will?

'The reasonings of mortals are unsure,

'And unstable our calculations.

'For the perishable body is a burden to the soul,

'The earthly tent hinders the concentration of the mind.

'We barely understand the things of this earth.

'Even what lies within our reach we have difficulty in finding.

'Who then can discover what is in Heaven?

'Or know Your Will, had You not granted Wisdom?

'Not sent from above Your Holy Spirit?

'Only thus will those on earth find straightened paths,

'Will men find out what pleases You,

'And are they saved by Wisdom'."

You may kneel down in your modern church.

You may do so in any Catholic church throughout the world.

Somewhere in it is a bright spot.

You know what it is: burning candles in front of the statue of Our Lady.

You are aware of their meaning: hearts burning in love, in sorrow, in agonizing anxieties, or in desperate struggle.

Each candle is a living heart left with Mary, calling for Her mercy.

Beside you people come and go.

They kneel in prayer.

Some with words, others speechless, few with tears, all ardent.

They call for Mary.

Centuries have called for Mary ...

We know our time.

We know too well how it lives, how it sins, how it prays.

It is worthwhile and instructive to know how ancient centuries have prayed, have prayed to Mary.

It is strengthening to see how the dust and the dusk of the past was lit up as the lighted spot in a Catholic church even in our own twentieth century.

The past prayed to Mary.

For the past has sinned too ...!

And it is from the past that we learn to pray:

" ... and protect me with Her glory ..."

"For Wisdom is quicker than anything that moves!"

What a magnificent assurance for a child of Mary, a child of the Holy Catholic Church in this day and age of revolt and apostasy, with all the terrible temptations to give in and follow suit. Yes, the Old Testament prayed to God, calling for Mary, who alone would have all the love and Wisdom necessary to give Her consent to our salvation!

VI

"Her resourceful ways, who knows them?"

"All Wisdom is from the Lord and it remains His own for ever.

Before all other things Wisdom was created,

and prudent understanding is everlasting.

To whom has Wisdom's origin ever been revealed?

Her resourceful ways, who knows them?

One only is wise, terrible indeed, seated on His throne: The Lord.

It is He who created Her, looked on Her and appraised Her worth,

And poured Her out on all His work to be with all mankind as His gift;

But He has lavished Her upon those who love Him."

These are the solemn words with which Jesus Ben Sirach opens for us in Chapter One, another biblical book of the wisdom literature - the book Ecclesiasticus. We will stay with this inspired author until the end of our own effort to learn whatever else God wishes to reveal "to those who love Him" about His beloved Wisdom.

From whatever angle we look at it, be it from the point of view of the majesty and veracity of God, or from the point of view of the intimate link and continuity between the Old Testament and the New Testament, or from the strength and the remarkable cohesion of the content itself of the text of the Wisdom literature, we must admit that, guided by the early Fathers and the liturgy of the Church, we have arrived at a very satisfactory answer to our prayerful investigation: 'What revelation did God have in Mind when He inspired the Wisdom texts?' Divine majesty requires that the reason is one of supreme importance for all times.

The intimate link and continuity between the Old Testament and the New Testament requires that a certain revelation in the New Testament gives the greatest possible explanation to what has been revealed in the Old. And the inner strength and cohesion of the Wisdom literature itself demand that the New Testament can only crown what had already been revealed in the Old. And crowns are only put on human heads.

God's dignity demands that His divine revelations are approached with the utmost respect. That they are not treated, or even brushed aside, as not being worthy of consideration, in preference to man made inventions and preconceived ideas, as the Modernists do. And especially that the impact of His revelation is not falsified due to an arbitrary and frivolous meaning being attached to His communications with the human race in general and His Chosen People in particular by means of His carefully selected authors and prophets.

Thus God, being the Author, Explainer and Guardian of His own revelations, has taken steps that His Authority, His Truth and His Protection would safely guide His message from the Old Testament to the New Testament, and would from then on be infallibly extended throughout history and the languages of the human race in the Tradition of the Holy Catholic Church. And it is in the fact that Catholic Tradition from its earliest beginning has applied the Wisdom literature to the Blessed Virgin Mary and to the One, Holy, Catholic and Apostolic Church created in Her image and likeness, that we find the reason why the Church now claims that this is part of God's veracity and purpose.

From the shocking way in which so many of our Modernist bishops, priests, 'theologians', religious and lay 'intellectuals' treat our Holy Mother the Catholic Church nowadays, that is, with the vilest possible contempt, it is timely to be reminded what God had revealed about 'the beginning of Wisdom', what He understands by 'Her Ways', and who has, and who has NOT, got access to Her. And if Modernists do not qualify on the score 'for finding Wisdom', then they also qualify for missing altogether both the Mother of God and the Holy Catholic Church. God's veracity, the cohesion of Scripture, and the inner strength and unity of what has been revealed all demand this continuity from the Old to the New, this transfer from 'Wisdom' to Mary, the acceptance of the Truth of what God has declared to be before Him as the ONE Reality. During the previous Five Days of our journey with Wisdom, we progressed from the way She was conceived by God in Eternity all the way to the mystical heights of 'Mount Carmel', where the 'hope of Israel' was inspired by God to implore Him for Her speedy arrival on earth.

So, what is left?

One of the two questions still outstanding for which Sacred Scripture will lay the foundation in this book of Wisdom literature is: WHY it was the purpose of Divine Wisdom, that so much of what God had revealed about 'created Wisdom', He in the Sacred Tradition of the Holy Catholic Church, directed personally towards the glorification of the Mother, when so much of it could have gone to the glorification of the Son. We recognise this as the bone of contention and the everlasting stumbling block of not a few Protestants and of all the Modernists; and thus as the unique possession of His One True Church. (Maybe that explains enough!)

The remaining question Sacred Scripture will address itself to is: HOW all 'the children of Wisdom' are in a most intimate relation with the Mother of God, and so with the Son and with each other.

The first question will be taken up now.

As already earlier made clear, it is by no means the purpose of this book to convey the impression that the Old Testament 'Wisdom' prefigures exclusively the Blessed Virgin Mary in the New Testament. All glory is ultimately only due to God 'Who created Her': to the Father, the Son and the Holy Spirit, and so to Jesus Christ, the only-begotten Son of God.

Rather it is much more a question of finding the <u>way</u> God Himself has revealed, which must be followed; in order that this glory due to Him can reach Him. It is out of reverence for God's revelation itself, out of acceptance of His known Will, and out of obedience to the infallible Tradition of the Holy Catholic Church He Himself called into being as the guardian of the totality of His revealed Truth, that we gladly and prayerfully follow the path traced out by Him along 'the ways of Wisdom' leading towards Him.

And so it is by His expressed wish, and due to the mystery of His own designs which He made known from the beginning, that this road to the glory of the Son goes only through His Holy Mother, the incomparable Virgin Mary. And, as Scripture reveals

"Only to the fool is this unbearable!
The undisciplined man will not stay with this for long!"

If Sacred Scripture can give so much glory to 'Wisdom', and if all Scripture is inspired by God, and so, cannot err, and if ultimately all glory is only due to God, then it is obvious that Sacred Scripture has no fear whatsoever that this glory bestowed by God on 'Wisdom' will in the end not be returned to God ...

By the same reasoning, if it is God's inscrutable design that 'Wisdom' prefigures Mary, and so passes on all glory given to Her in the Old Covenant to the Blessed Virgin Mary in the New, then neither God nor Sacred Scripture show any concern whatsoever that, in the course of this transfer, some glory due to God would not reach Him. And if God shows no such fear, then, as the Book of Ecclesiasticus continues, we are well advised 'to fear God' sufficiently NOT to insult Him by holding this, our own private fear, up to Him as being inspired by Him. The unholy fear, that is, by honouring the Mother, we may detract from the Son.

"To fear the Lord is the beginning of Wisdom.
She was formed with His elect in their mothers' womb.
She has made Her abode with devoted men from of old,
And with their children Her beneficence remains.
To fear the Lord is the perfection of Wisdom.
She intoxicates them with Her fruits;

She fills their whole house with their hearts' desire,
And their storeroom with Her produce.
The fear of the Lord is the crown of Wisdom,
It makes peace and health to flourish.
The Lord has looked on Her and assessed Her;
She showers down knowledge and full understanding,
And exalts the glory of those who hold Her close.
Yes, the fear of the Lord is the beginning of Wisdom,
And Her branches are eternal Life."

With this, God has been placed safely at the beginning and at the end of Wisdom: Her 'beginning' and Her 'crown' and at anywhere in the middle Her 'perfection'. So there is no fear then, that 'Wisdom' will allow Her children to corrupt this beautiful harmony by diverting some of that glory to Herself. Whenever or wherever that may occur, it is certainly not inspired by 'Wisdom', but comes from the 'Evil one', whence also comes the Protestant and Modernist practise of withholding glory from God due to Him through 'Wisdom', for fear that such glory would not reach Him! Divine revelation has made it clear that it is God Himself Who will never allow this to happen; nor that He will ever allow that this 'fear' could at any time be legitimately claimed in name of Wisdom!

It is obvious that here in the Old Testament a firm foundation is being laid for something very important in the New. If Old Testament Jews could safely pray for the fullest possible share of Wisdom because of all the blessings the Divine Creator had adorned this exquisite creature with, so, because of the divinely willed transfer to the New, love for the Holy Mother of God and for the Holy Catholic Church will never be in danger of detracting from God unless sins of imprudence and presumption enter the picture to cause the detracting. And that, when all is said and done, is selfishness, not 'Wisdom'. For 'Her Ways' never lead one to selfishness, not even sin, as will be made clear very soon.

And so the human instrument of this stream of divine revelations goes on:

"My son, from your earliest youth embrace discipline,
And till your hair is white you will keep finding Wisdom.
Approach Her like the ploughman and the sower,
And then wait for Her fine harvest.
For in Her service you will toil only a little,
but very soon you will be eating Her fruits.

- Only to the fool is She unbearable,
- The undisciplined man does not stay with Her for long:
- She will weigh on him like a heavy stone
- And he will lose no time in throwing Her off.

But you, my son, put your feet into Her fetters
And your neck into Her harness.
Put your shoulders under Her yoke and carry Her,
And be not irked by Her bonds.
Yes, approach Her with all your soul,
And keep Her ways with all your might.
Go after Her and seek Her and She will reveal Herself to you.

Once you hold Her do not let Her go,
For in the end you will find rest in Her,
And she will be your joy.
Her fetters will be your strong defence.
Her harness a robe of honour.
Her yoke will be a golden ornament,
Her reins, purple ribbons.
You will wear Her like a mantle of honour,
Bear Her like a magnificent crown."

If ever an Old Testament Jew reading this needed convincing that, in seeking after Wisdom, he was literally 'seeking after God', then the little sentence slipped in here by the Holy Spirit would have the desired result:

"Yes, approach Her with all your soul,
And keep Her ways with all your might."

For these words would have been a vivid reminder to him of Moses' command, contained in the Book of Deuteronomy:

"Listen, Israel, the Lord our God is the one Lord, and you must love the Lord your God with all your heart, with all your soul, with all your mind and with all your strength." (Dt. 6: 4-5)

If this famous quote from the Book of Deuteronomy guaran-tees that this great union between 'Wisdom' and God in no way detracts from the glory due to God alone, and that this great union is not only acceptable to God, but is willed by God, so it can be written up as a command, then looking into the New Testament over the boundary of the Old, we may appreciate that here we have come across the root cause why God made 'love for Mary' a condition for His service in the New.

In the Old Testament nothing – as we saw – would make love of Wisdom evaporate more quickly than 'being undisciplined', which in practical language meant falling away from service of the One True God into idolatry and grave sins of sexual immorality. Idolatry was the evil practise of serving a 'man-made God' in any kind of 'man-made religion'. If during the long periods of such religious and sexual aberrations the infidel Jew managed to maintain some sort of tenuous illusion of 'service to God', then it is obvious that 'service of God' was not necessarily the immediate criterium which would distinguish an apostate from a law abiding Jew. And there can be little doubt in our minds that God, in order to break this illusion, had provided His 'headstrong people' with a more convincing way to sort out the mess. And that, according to the Divine Mind, the realisation amongst His wayward children "that 'the Ways of Wisdom' have been abandoned" in such undisciplined behaviour, was meant to be a more realistic and simple (and consequently a more effective) 'early-warning-system' against apostasy than the realisation that the ways of the Law had been abandoned.

What has this got to do with us? Plenty!

Down through the ages the Church founded by Christ would suffer the agony of breakaways from Her unity. The sects so formed would build their own 'sanctuaries' for use in their own 'man-made religions', claiming them to be the ones built by God. Something would be salvaged from the shipwreck which resembles some part of the Mother Church, but never structures such as 'pillars', or foundations. And so the ongoing illusion would be maintained by all breakaways that somehow 'the church' is being continued in a new way, and that somehow God is pleased with the new 'service'. So again, as in the days of the Jewish apostasy, 'God', 'religion', 'church' and 'service' are NOT necessarily the criteria which make it immediately clear to the breakaways that they have left the One True Church, that they have started their own man-made religion and that God is certainly NOT pleased with the latest 'service'.

Such behaviour in the New Testament is truly as undisciplined as Jewish apostasy in the Old, and so it is no wonder that God illuminates this periodic abandoning of 'The Ways of Wisdom' in the New Testament with the same 'Reflection of the Eternal Light': His Holy Mother (even in our days) as He used to draw attention to the undisciplined behaviour in the Old Covenant by pointing out the stark difference of the 'new ways' with the 'Ways of Wisdom'.

So, unless Christ sees indelibly engraved on the pillars of a sanctuary the Name of His Holy Mother, He will not recognise the pillars, and consequently will not acknowledge the 'sanctuary' as the one of His Father. And History has borne Him out on this stroke of divine genius: NONE of the breakaways have ever taken with them a great and lasting devotion to the Blessed Virgin Mary any more than the Jewish apostates took with them a great and lasting love for Wisdom into their 'new religions'. In fact, Our Blessed Lady was always the first to be deserted, the first to be 'banished into the desert' of oblivion. "They did not lose time in throwing Her off", showing that, in the Mind of God, such breakaways from the Holy Catholic Church are considered 'fools': "Only to the fool is She unbearable. The undisciplined man does not stay with Her for long!"

And because of the divine command:

"Yes, approach Her 'with all your soul',
And keep Her ways 'with all your might'",

which we recognise as the command Moses gave the sons of Israel as their supreme obligation in the service of Yahweh, then there is no way known that, because of this intimate relationship between God and His Holy Mother, and between God and His Holy Church, that breakaways from this 'Marian Church', those who refuse to obey the command "to approach both the Mother and Her Daughter with all their soul", and "to keep Her Ways with all their might", that such people can never legitimately claim 'to serve God' or to start a 'church' or a 'religion' pleasing to Him.

Fervent, true, genuine, traditional and lasting devotion for the Mother of God, i.e. the acceptance of, and to glory in, what the present Holy Father Pope John Paul II has graced several times with the name 'the Marian Dimension' in his 1987 Encyclical, Redemptorist Mater, will be recognised by Christ as the hallmark of the true Sanctuary in which He dwells. And the prize for this can only go to ONE Church.

And now we know for sure why <u>all</u> the Catholic Modernists of our time are doomed for holding up their man-made 'church' with its man-made 'religion' as 'catholic': It is a 'church' and a 'religion' without Mary! And in their determination to inflict this very great evil on us, they show how 'undisciplined' they have become, and how they are now 'fools' in the sight of God.

VII

"... and selects Her as his nextdoor neighbour"

And now at last, in the Divine Mind, we are ready for the myriad of blessings attached to the service of 'Wisdom'.

"Blessed the man who is mindful of Wisdom,
And who sets himself to acquire understanding.
Who ponders 'Her Ways' in his heart,
And takes the study of Her Mysteries seriously."

Yes, infinite blessings on all those who, through the inestimable gift of a great love for the Mother of God, have come to acquire an equally great love for their Holy Mother the Catholic Church, and of the pearl of great beauty within Her, the priceless gift of their Catholic Faith.

Blessed all those fallen children of Eve who, because of the acquisition of this great dual love, have heeded the Church's laws of chastity inside and outside marriage: all those 'who were not irked by Her bonds', but 'kept Her Ways with all their might', and now, in the age of rampant AIDS, have found out to their great consolation, that 'Her fetters DID become their strong defence', and that indeed 'Her reins ARE the purple ribbons of victory'.

And does not the unbreakable bond between Mother and Daughter not shine out in that glorious line of Priests who, during those arduous centuries, have "acquired the understanding" that a great devotion to Our Blessed Lady became for them the most indispensable grace to keep the laws of celibacy of the Holy Catholic Church?

And then, what Marian Catholic would fail to see in these quoted lines:

> "Who ponders 'Her Ways' in his heart,
> and takes the study of Her Mysteries seriously."

the biblical roots and the divinely inspired confirmation of the Holy Rosary? Yes indeed, let us start anew this long list of blessings heaped on those who appear to the world to have only eyes for their Holy Mother the Catholic Church. Because by some mysterious harmony, pre-ordained in Eternity, they seem to be chiming in with Revelation in such a unique way that, far from being blind for the needs of their times as their 'popular' Modernist and Teilhardian contemporaries accuse them of being, they show by their whole life that, like Our Blessed Lady at Cana, they have discovered the secret of Heaven of contemplating <u>everything</u> through the eyes of God and of their heavenly Mother.

> "Blessed the man who is mindful of Wisdom,
> And who sets himself to acquire understanding.
> Who ponders Her ways in his heart,
> And takes the study of Her Mysteries seriously.
> Who pursues Her like a scout,
> And lies in wait by Her paths.
> Who looks in on Her through Her windows,

And listens at Her doors.
Who lodges close to Her house,
And drives his tent pins in Her walls.
Such a man pitches his tent at Her side,
And selects Her as his nextdoor neighbour.
He builds his nest in Her foliage,
And lodges in her branches.
He is sheltered by Her from the heat, *
Her home has become his refuge.
Whoever fears the Lord will act like this,
And whoever practices the Law shall find Wisdom."
(* the heat of temptations)

We may be forgiven for interrupting here for a moment the biblical visions of future Catholics with respect to Our Blessed Lady and the Catholic Church, by drawing attention once more to the cohesion and the essential unity of biblical inspiration:

"Whoever fears <u>the Lord</u> will act like this with Wisdom!"
Which is for us a vivid reminder of what went before:
"The fear of <u>the Lord</u> is the beginning, the perfection and the
   crown of <u>Wisdom</u>."

The wisdom: to love Wisdom; to keep 'Her Ways'; to find 'Her most sure beginning in discipline'. Why is it written that 'God loves only those who live with Wisdom'? Why this God-inspired 'identification' between Himself and Wisdom, when we read 'approach Her with all your soul, and keep Her Ways with all your might', when it is also written that we must "love the Lord our God with all our heart, with all our soul, with all our mind and with all our strength"?

Because 'Wisdom leads to immortality'. 'To sovereignty'. Because Wisdom does not divert one iota to Herself, but leads to love of Him. Because whatever lies revealed in 'Wisdom', leads ultimately to Him.

And so in a most literal sense, we have been warned time and time again, that we do not show 'fear of the <u>Lord</u>' if we do not take His revelations of 'the Mysteries of <u>Wisdom</u>' seriously! Divine Mysteries which extend across the border far into the New Covenant in His Blood ...

> "Whoever fears the Lord will act like this,
> And whoever practices the Law shall find Wisdom.
> Like a Mother She will come out and meet him,
> And receive him as the bride of his youth.
> She will give him the bread of understanding to eat,
> And the water of Wisdom to drink.
> He can lean on Her without faltering,
> Rely on Her and not be put to shame.
> She will raise him high above his neighbours,
> Open his mouth in full assembly.
> She will fill him with the Spirit of Wisdom and Intellect.
> And clothe Him in a magnificent garment.
> Happiness and joy will be his,
> As She will win for him an everlasting reputation."

These – in the sight of the inspiring God – are the glories and blessings of being a Catholic, to which will be added the extra glories and blessings of being consciously a 'child of Mary', when, through the recitation of the daily Rosary, 'they ponder Her Ways in their hearts and take the study of Her Mysteries seriously', 'and are sheltered by Her from the heat of temptations'.

VIII

"They who make Me their concern will never sin"

It has been a real feast. But, as with all God's revelations, the joy of unfolding each mystery seems to be never ending. What have we been privileged to receive? We were shown the origin of Wisdom, Her inner beauty, Her strength and authority. We learned about 'Her Ways', Her riches and privileges, and about all Her manifold blessings. Now we are fortunate to be present when Wisdom Herself will disclose the most profound reason the Divine Creator had in Mind for revealing all Her splendour in the Old Dispensation, in plenty of time for His Divine Revelations in the New. As with Our Lady's intervention at Cana, the best wine is being kept till the end and, as with Our Lady's Magnificat at the home of Elizabeth, Wisdom Herself is allowed to introduce the necessary setting

"Wisdom is about to speak Her own praises,
Before Her own people She proclaims Her Glory.
In the Assembly of the Most High She opens Her mouth,
To declare Her worth before His host.
In the midst of the Elect She will speak of Her renown,
And exalt Her glory among the Blessed." *

(* A clear reference to Mary's Magnificat, and the greeting of Elizabeth.)

221

So 'fools' are not invited. No provision here for those 'who lost no time in throwing Her off'. 'Undisciplined apostates' who 'lost Her Ways' and so started their own 'religions' in 'sanctuaries' not graced with pillars displaying Her Name, are barred forever!

- 'Fools' do not belong to 'Her own People'.
- Those 'who threw Her off' are not found in 'the Assembly of the Most High'.
- Those 'who became undisciplined; and lost Her Ways' are no longer 'His host'.
- Those who start their own 'religion' in 'sanctuaries' not 'graced with the Name of this exquisite Mother' have vacated their place 'in the midst of the Elect'.
- And all those who have 'chased the Woman into the desert of oblivion' have forfeited forever the glory of being counted 'among the blessed'.

What comfort can a modern 'fool', a Modernist 'catholic' of our days find in all this? What good is now the pretense that '<u>She</u> was cast off to please <u>God</u>'? What is being said here is divine revelation, yet who is 'about to speak'? Not God, but 'the One who so often is thrown off and chased into the desert'! But She is most definitely declaring here with the Authority of God who are 'the Elect', and who are the ones rejected by God! Here, by letting Wisdom declare with His authority who will, and who will not, be in His presence, the infinite Wisdom of God Himself is being vindicated when, after the Fall he established the 'Everlasting Enmity' NOT between Himself and Satan but between 'the Woman and Her

Seed' and 'you and yours', so that from then on 'this Woman' should have the authority to speak 'on His behalf'.

What else can this be than the glorious foundations of the 'Marian Church' being revealed to exist here in the Old Testament at the foundations of Wisdom!

We have now come to the root-question WHY God built this magnificent mansion for Wisdom in the Old Testament to be extended for co-habitation with His Marian Church in the New, gracing both occupants with His own Authority. How exactly is the Church founded by Christ to be Marian, and how does Wisdom explain this? We have come to appreciate that, because Our Lady and the Holy Catholic Church refer directly to an exclusive Reality in the Old Testament: Wisdom, they must be strongly related in the New, but how? How can a Holy Father claim that "in the Liturgy the Church salutes Mary of Nazareth as the Church's OWN BEGINNING"? How does Christ fit in with all this?

As St. Paul has revealed, it was contained in the inscrutable Decree taken by the Blessed Trinity from all eternity "that the Second Person of the adorable Trinity, the Son of the eternal Father, should redeem the human race not merely as an individual, but AS THE HEAD OF A BODY" (Eph. 1: 1-14). The Decree means that for its fulfillment, Our Blessed Lord at the moment of His Incarnation had to be "fitted" with TWO bodies: a physical one that made Him Human, and a mystical one that made HIM HEAD. No one but Mary could, at this moment, give Her WISE consent to the twofold aspects of the one Decree. That is, first in Her own name, so that, as the 'New Eve' of the redemption, She could 'fit' Him with the Mystical Body that made Him Head. In order that She could give Her consent freely and most worthily, it was necessary that the Blessed Virgin Mary was fully aware that She was asked by God TO BE that Second Body, that Mystical Body, the one that made Our Saviour "the Head of all mankind as well as of His Body, the Church". And furthermore that SHE HERSELF, as the beginning of that Mystical Body, would have to unite Herself, as the Body to the Head, with all the sufferings that would be endured by that other body which She had been asked to give to God, the one that made Him Human. So that is the reason why a future Pope could write:

"Within Her virginal womb Christ Our Lord already bore the exalted title of Head of the Church". (Pius XII, 'The Mystical Body of Christ and our union in it with Christ', 1943)

And why another future Pope could write:

"In the liturgy, the Church salutes Mary of Nazareth as the Church's own beginning." (John Paul II in 'Redemptorist Mater'. 1987)

For, at one blessed moment in time, Mary was the WHOLE Church, the WHOLE Mystical Body, the only member united to the Head, Christ; just as in one unforgettable moment in history EVE in her single body, united the WHOLE human race to her head, Adam. And that is how the Fall became 'a corporate affair' in which the whole of humanity fell from Grace in only two of its members: its head Adam, and his consenting body, Eve. In the same way did the Redemption become 'a corporate affair' in which grace was restored to the whole human race by a unique, but this time sinless, Pair: a Head, the New Adam, and His consenting body, the New Eve.

And just as the spiritual death of Adam's guilt was passed on from the head through Eve to all her children as the Original Sin, so it is also that the 'fullness of grace' found in the Head Jesus Christ, in its totality flows first through the Blessed Virgin Mary to reach all the other members of the Church founded by Christ, and through this Marian Church into the whole world, but through no other member of this Church any more in its totality. Which makes Our Lady the "Mediatrix of ALL graces". (Pope St. Pius X. *Ad Diem Illum*, 1904)

> "Wisdom is about to speak Her own praises,
> Before Her own people She proclaims Her Glory.
> In the Assembly of the Most High She opens Her mouth,
> To declare Her worth before His host.
> In the midst of the Elect She will speak of Her renown,
> And exalt Her glory among the Blessed.
> 'I came forth from the mouth of the Most High,
> 'And covered the earth like a mist.
> 'I had My tent in the heights,
> 'My throne in a pillar of cloud.
> 'Alone I encircled the vault of the sky,
> 'And walked the deep of the abyss,
> 'The waves of the sea, the whole earth,
> 'To reveal My power to every people and nation'.

'Among all these I searched for rest,
'An inheritance where I could remain'."

Here Wisdom is obviously sent forth by God to scout around for a future home where a permanent love and devotion would flourish for Her whom She prefigured, the Mother of God. And just as Wisdom finally took root in the Jewish people, so Our Blessed Lady found Her home with Her children within the Church founded by Her Son, the Holy Catholic Church.

"'Then the Creator of all gave Me His command,
'And He who wrought Me decided the place for My tent,
'And He said: "In Jacob will be Your abode, make Israel Your
    inheritance".
'Before the ages, from the beginning created by Him.
'I will remain for eternity.
'I ministered before Him in His holy Tabernacle.
'And thus I became established in Zion.
'He made Me live in His beloved city,
'In Jerusalem is My dominion.
'Thus I took root in a privileged people,
'In the Lord's property, in the midst of His inheritance.
'I rose as a cedar on Lebanon,
'As a cypress on Mount Hermon.
'I have grown tall as a palm in Engedi,
'As the rosebushes of Jericho,
'As a fine olive in the plain,
'Like a plane tree growing along a stream.

'Like cinnamon, or balm or precious myrrh,

'I gave forth perfume.

'Like galbanum, and onycha and sweet spices,

'Like the odour of incense in the holy place.

'I spread My branches like a terebinth,

'My branches so glorious and graceful.

(Who does not think of First Communicants here, prepared by
     Nuns who truly resemble the Blessed Virgin Mary …)

'I am like a vine putting out graceful shoots,

'Whose blossoms bear fruits of glory and wealth.

'I am the Mother of pure love,

'Of fear, of knowledge and of holy hope.

'In Me is all grace of life and truth,

'In Me is all hope for life and virtue.

'Come to Me, you who desire Me,

'And be filled with My fruits.

'Thinking of Me is sweeter than honey,

'Inheriting Me is sweeter than the honeycomb.

'Whosoever will eat Me will hunger for more.

'They who drink Me will thirst for more.

'Whoever listens to Me will never have reason to blush;

'They who make Me their concern will never sin'."

"They who make Me their concern will never sin."

What an astounding promise! What a declaration in the face of
the world of our times! And what a challenge for the rising chorus
of satanists in preparation for the reign of Antichrist!

A challenge for those 'who lost no time in throwing Her off': Catholics who took the mark of the Beast; who drove Mary and the Church from their contraceptive 'life-styles' only to become 'psycho babblers', no longer making any sense.

A grave challenge to Priests-who-want-to-be-married and to 'nuns'-who-want-to-be-priests, who are changing the structures of the Church only to find themselves operating in 'sanctuaries' no longer graced with the presence of either the Mother or Daughter: 'fools' all of them, "who will never understand", according to the great prophet Daniel.

"They who make Me their concern will never sin."

Who are those 'who make Me their concern'?

Only those 'who live with Wisdom', who 'disciplined themselves' in order to find 'Hers Ways', or, as it is revealed here:

- 'Her own people',
- 'the Assembly of the Most High',
- Those who are 'His host',
- who are found 'in the midst of the Elect',
- and who find it of the utmost importance to be counted 'among the Blessed'.

the 'Saints' St. John describes in his Book of Revelation, God's very own, those "who will follow the Lamb wherever It goes", those "on which 'the Beast' will make war", but "who will never have reason to blush": who will never have cause to be ashamed of their Faith and trust in their beloved Catholic Church and its beloved Virgin!

"No first man ever grasped Her entirely.

No last one will fully comprehend Her.

For richer than the sea is Her knowledge,

Richer than the great ocean Her comprehension.

More abundantly than the morning light will I make Wisdom
     shine forth.

I shall send Her light far and wide;

I shall pour out Her teaching like a prophecy,

A legacy for all future generations.

Observe that I do not toil for myself alone,

But for all those who are seeking Wisdom."

Words inspired by God, Who can maintain, in the face of all this, that God is not honoured when Wisdom is given so much glory!

IX

"That's why, in Her, I acquired
a priceless possession"

The last day of this novena, the end of the road. But like all endings, what a beginning! Wisdom's invitation to a life of union with God through love for Our Lady and for a holy Church of which She is the spotless beginning. An ending and a beginning inspired by the Holy Spirit of God Himself, before Whom, all else falls silent,

"When I was still young, before I went travelling,

I asked outright for Wisdom in my prayers.

Outside the entrance to the Sanctuary I would pray for Her,

And did not cease to yearn for Her.

She blossomed inside me as a ripening grape,

And in Her my heart found its delight.

My foot followed the path of Her Truth,

I have been following Her steps ever since my youth.

By bowing my ear a little I have received Her,

And have found much instruction.

Thanks to Her I have advanced:

Glory to Him Who gave me Wisdom.

Looking for Her I would not allow myself any rest;

I was not put to shame, for I have found Her.

My soul adhered to Her from then on,

I sought Her out in all my actions.

My hand opened Her gate,

I went in and I gazed on Her."

Who, on reading these immortal words, would not be compelled to think here of Cardinal Newman, or any of the great English converts? Or of the mysterious force by which millions upon millions of nameless souls found their way into the Catholic Church!

Yes, we finally made our way in the presence of Her whom sinner and Saint, in agony and ecstasy, has graced with the everlasting name: Our Holy Mother the Catholic Church. Like Our Lady, the Church grew in years but never wrinkled. She is still the youthful, spotless Bride of the Lamb of God, the Holy One, the Faithful One. Over the centuries She has done what Her Divine Founder and Groom had wanted Her to do: to bear Him children, many children; to fill 'His Father's House' from the ends of the earth.

She instructed them in purity of doctrine, in poverty of spirit, in obedience to the Father's word. And the Son of God loved Her. He adorned Her with His most precious jewels, He entrusted to Her care His most priceless possessions: His Body, His Blood, His Grace, His Heart, His Truth, His infinite Mercy, the Mysteries of His Divine Knowledge, the Honour of His Holy Mother. He cared for Her as never a groom cared for a bride.

And in return the Church loved the Lamb of God with an eternity of love. For Him She loved the sinner as much as the Saint. She taught the ignorant as well as the learned. She strengthened the Martyr to stand form till the end. She consoled the bereaved, prepared the dying, and cared for the poor and the sick, the orphan and the widow, the heathen and the lost. She was all to all. She will never be under the control of iniquity nor under the command of men. She can live under any system, outlast any enemy, survive any evil. For the Church does not rest on human counsels nor on the councils of the world. Her Head is divine, so is Her Life. She has no need to speak with the voice of this world to be heard.

For within Her is the pearl of great beauty for which the merchant-in-the-know sacrificed everything in order to possess it: Catholic Faith, the most precious gift of Almighty God to finite little man. For it is through that Faith, and that Faith alone, that we know Him, His Son and His Holy Spirit; His Mother, His Church and the Bodily presence of His Son in the Blessed Eucharist; and also his Face in the poor, and His Truth in Humanae Vitae.

Catholic Faith will never die out on earth. It will never disappear from this earth. It will never cease to have consequences on this earth: fruits of Redemption and eternal Salvation. Fruits of prayer and penance, of great Hope and great Love. Fruits of conversion to Her from whom this Faith was received in the first place: Our Holy Mother the Catholic Church.

"With all my soul I resolved to follow Her,
And in purity I have found Her.
Having obtained understanding from Her from the beginning,
I shall never desert Her.
My very core was burning to discover Her,
That's why, in Her, I acquired a priceless possession.
Come close to me, you uninstructed,
And stay for a while in my school.

For how much longer will you suffer the lack of all this,
While your souls are so thirsty for it?
Buy yourselves Wisdom without money,
Bow your necks under Her yoke,
Let your souls carry Her burden.
She is never far from those who yearn for Her,
And he who gives his soul to Her, will find Her.
See for yourselves how slight my efforts have been,
And how great the peace I found in Her ..."

No mortal can improve on these immortal words, or hope to add to their divine impact. And so we will end our 'Novena of Quotes' on this crystal clarity, remembering it comes to us from "the reflection of Eternal Light."

X

"The 'New Eve'"

The author of this little volume is fully aware of these words of the Apostle of the Gentiles:

"This is what I pray, kneeling before the Father, from whom every family, whether spiritual or natural, takes its name:

Out of His infinite glory, may He give you the power through His Spirit for your hidden self to grow strong, so that Christ may live in your hearts through faith. And then, planted in love and built on love, you will with all the Saints have strength to grasp the breadth and the length, the height and the depth; until knowing the love of Christ, which is beyond all knowledge, you are filled with the utter fullness of God.

Glory be to Him whose power, working in us, can do infinitely more than we can ask or imagine; glory to Him from generation to generation in the Church and in Christ Jesus for ever and ever. Amen." (Eph. 3 : 14-21)

The author is equally fully aware that, over the centuries, evil forces have been at work, and are still at work today according to Pope St. Pius X in 'Our Apostolic Mandate', 1910, to seduce Catholics to fit these words somehow into a 'church' of their own making, in separation from the Holy Church for the acceptance and spread of which the great St. Paul had been labouring until his martyrdom.

For anything that God had revealed at any time for the full recognition of this unique Church is contained in "the breadth and the length, the height and the depth" which St. Paul wanted the Christians of all times "to grasp". And since every separating 'sect' would be at great pains to convince itself and to 'prove' to others that it took Christ with it into its 'RENEWED church', then it does not take the genius of St. Paul to understand the Evil One had succeeded in preventing Christ from remaining the criterium by which a separating 'church' could be distinguished from the True Church.

But, as this little book has shown, God had taken His precautions 'from the beginning', ever since, at the time of the Fall, He had established the 'Everlasting Enmity' NOT between Himself and Satan, but between 'The Woman and Her children' and 'You and your seed', as the infallible foundation for the permanent recognition of the Mother Church. Slowly, the details of God's eternal decrees were allowed to become revealed, until in the pages of the Wisdom literature of the Old Testament, the full thrust of the Divine Designs for a foolproof recognition of His future Church became unfolded.

Must we not admit that it is to the everlasting glory of the genius of the divine Architect, that His unfolding of the foolproof recognition of the Mother Church in the pages of the Old Dispensation became at the same time the unfolding of a very unique and singular glory it had been given to the Old Testament to bestow 'in advance' on the Blessed Virgin Mary, "the Beginning, the Mother and the Model" of this Church?

Many are the glories that can be laid at the doorstep of 'The House of Gold', the House that Divine Wisdom had built for Itself: the glory of Her Immaculate Conception, the glory of Her Divine Motherhood, and the glory of Her perpetual virginity. Yet, no matter how great and varied the light is that issues forth from these pearls in Mary's crown, there is still room for more.

How do we know this for sure?

From the fact that the Dogma of Mary's bodily assumption into Heaven was not traced by the defining Pontiff 'to the sources of Revelation' along the path of any of these stupendous privileges. According to the infallible pronouncement in which the latest of the Marian dogmas lies expressed, of all the glorious titles that two thousand years of Christianity had gathered together for the adornment of the sacred person of the Blessed Virgin Mary, those three main ones just mentioned could only be accepted as 'fitting' reasons for Mary's bodily assumption into heaven, but were not considered sufficiently cogent reasons to build this new Marian Dogma on.

Yet Christianity had always believed in the bodily assumption of the Blessed Virgin Mary into heaven. Along what path then could this firm and constant belief be traced 'to the sources of Revelation' so it could become the foundation of yet another 'Revealed Truth' concerning the Mother of God? What had God revealed about the Blessed Virgin Mary 'in the sources of Revelation': Sacred Scripture, and had, on His divine command, been taught by the Apostles to the Early Church, that was not included in Mary's Immaculate Conception, Her Divine Maternity, Her Perpetual Virginity?

At the time of the solemn definition, all Christianity was holding its breath, especially after Europe's 'leading theologian' had declared with consummate audacity "that the Pope could save himself the trouble of defining this new Marian Dogma, as the bodily assumption of the Virgin Mary into heaven 'could not be traced to the sources of Revelation'".

But not even a ton of good theology can produce a grain of Supernatural, Infused, Divine and Catholic Faith, let alone a whole sewer of what the modernists understand by 'their new theology'. Guided not by theology nor 'theology', but by the power and light of the Holy Spirit, Pope Pius XII went ahead and declared the bodily Assumption of the Blessed Virgin Mary a "Truth revealed by God, a Dogma of the Church, to be believed by all Catholics for their eternal salvation".

And that was that, leading 'theologian' or not.

Perhaps the best way to answer our question: "What had God revealed about the Blessed Virgin Mary in the sources of Revelation, Sacred Scripture, and had been communicated to the Early Church, that was not included in Mary's other great privileges?" by quoting the defining Pontiff, Pope Pius XII, from the Constitution "Munificentissimus Deus" of 1950, in which the Holy Father not only gave to the whole Church the Dogma of Mary's Assumption into heaven, but also traced for us the roots of this Dogma to the sources of Revelation.

"We must remember especially that, since the second century, the Virgin Mary has been designated by the holy Fathers as the new Eve, who, although subject to the new Adam, is most intimately associated with him in that struggle against the infernal foe which, as foretold in the protoevangelium, would finally result in that most complete victory over the sin and death which are always mentioned together in the writings of the Apostle of the Gentiles. Consequently, just as the glorious resurrection of Christ was an essential part and the final sign of this victory, so that struggle which was common to the Blessed Virgin and her divine Son should be brought to a close by the glorification of her virginal body, for the same Apostle says: 'When this mortal thing hath put on immortality, then shall come to pass the saying that is written: Death is swallowed up in victory'." (1 Cor 15:54.) (#39)

The full force of the papal teaching springs to light from the Latin text: "the glorification of Her Virginal body HAD TO FOLLOW!" And on what did the Holy Father place this necessity? On only ONE thing: on a COMMON STRUGGLE. "... that struggle which was common to the Blessed Virgin Mary and Her Divine Son".

In the first 38 numbers of the Constitution the Holy Father shows that he was well aware of all that 1900 years of Tradition had taught on the Assumption of Our Blessed Lady. Mentioning and bypassing all the fitting reasons for Catholic belief in Our Lady's glorious Assumption, Pope Pius XII broke new ground in No. 39. Here at last he came to the crux of the whole matter: on what facts, revealed in Revelation and contained in Sacred Scripture was the NECESSITY of this solemn doctrine founded, if it could not be based on reasons which were merely 'fitting' for it to be declared a Dogma of the Church, no matter how dogmatically true the fitting reasons were in themselves?

The Dogma of Mary's Assumption body and soul into heaven is not based by the defining Holy Father on any of Her privileges. It is not based on Her Immaculate Conception. Nor is it based on Her Divine Motherhood, or Her Perpetual Virginity. It is really not based by the Pope on anything that God had done for Her: it is strictly speaking based on what Mary did for God! It is squarely based here by the defining Holy Father on Her absolutely free choice to go beyond the call of mere duty to that of VICTIM-HOOD: to be the 'New Eve' with the New Adam. It was this <u>neces-sity</u>: "that at the moment of the Incarnation the Son of God as the 'New Adam', should be freely fitted not only with His Human Body but also with that other Body, His Mystical Body, the one that made Him Head of all Humanity and of the Church", which was contained in the Decree of Predestination. And just as only one helpmate was given to Adam in Paradise for the dual role of becoming herself 'the mother of all the living' and of making him head of the human race, so here too, in the Eternal Decree of Pre-destination, there was room for only <u>one</u> Woman, 'the Woman of Genesis', to be asked by God to give Her consent to be <u>both</u> the Mother of the Son as well as His Helpmate in the work of Redemp-tion. For the defining Pontiff continued:

"Hence the revered Mother of God, 'from all eternity joined in a hidden way with Jesus Christ in one and the same decree of pre-destination', ... finally obtained ... that she should be preserved free from the corruption of the tomb ..." (#40)

The quoted words in this text 'from all eternity joined ...' were taken by Pope Pius XII from the Bull "Ineffabilis Deus", in which his predecessor Pope Pius IX had declared and formulated the

Dogma of the Immaculate Conception almost a century before, in 1854.

Here two Holy Father's almost a century apart, in two documents of the Church carrying supreme weight as they deal with two Marian Dogmas, in tracing these Dogmas to the sources of Revelation have declared with the Authority of Christ Himself, that Mary 'has a share in that supreme Decree', and that not only She was predestined to be the Mother of God, but also His Bride. To be the beginning of that other Body of Christ, His Mystical Body, the Church, of which Christ is the Head. And in consenting to BOTH aspects of this SAME Decree of Predestination, Mary consented to 'stand in for all Humanity', and to reverse, through Her obedience and Her suffering, what Eve had lost through disobedience and self-gratification. And since the defining Pontiff had to reach beyond the New Testament deep into the Old to give to the 'necessity' contained in the Decree the meaning it needed for it to become the foundation for a Dogma of the Church, so the all-knowing God had already considerably extended both the meaning and the foundation of the future glorification of His 'New Eve' by giving infallible inspiration to the Old Testament Wisdom literature.

In God's infinite designs therefore, ONE Woman, the 'Woman of Genesis', should be at once the Mother and a Virgin, the Mother of God and the Bride of God, should be Immaculate from the moment of Her Conception and go through life without a stain of personal sin, yet as the 'New Eve' alongside Her Son should suffer more for sinners, and for the redemption from sin, than would ever be asked of any sinner or Saint who ever lived.

Had this most recent of the Marian Dogmas, that of Mary's Assumption into Heaven, been traced 'to the sources of Revelation' along the part of any of the other Marian Dogmas, or what is the same, would have had as its foundation Mary's Divine Motherhood, or Her Perpetual Virginity, or Her Immaculate Conception, each of them fitting reasons for a triumphant entry into glory, then history would have counted many disillusioned sinners who, while mentally admitting 'that of course such an elevated and privileged creature is in Heaven', may nevertheless have succumbed in their innermost hearts to a temptation of despondency of feeling 'that in Her exalted state, Mary was beyond their reach'.

What an immense debt of gratitude then all Christendom owes God on behalf of all the nameless sinners, that the guiding Light of the Holy Spirit had blocked any of these three paths for being the foundation of the Dogma of Mary's entry into glory. And that instead the glory of the Divine Motherhood, offered exclusively to 'the Woman of Genesis', could only be reached through the narrow gate of intense personal suffering, associated with this Woman being at the same time the 'New Eve' to 'the Man of sorrow'. For any sinner in history can relate to Mary 'standing under the cross of Her divine Son' if it is realised that She was there "standing in" on behalf of each one of us in obedience to the Eternal Decree of Predestination containing the conditions for our salvation: that the 'New Eve' should make up in Her own sinless body "what was lacking in the sufferings of Christ for His body the Church". And that HERE, under the cross of Her dying Son, She displayed publicly for all generations to come, that She truly is the beginning, the Mother and the Model of the only Church founded by Her Son in Her spotless image and likeness. And it is for the teaching of this unique Marian Church:

> "That thus, in Her new Motherhood in the Spirit, Mary embraces each and everyone in THIS Church and embraces each and everyone through THIS Church."

That we could give to this little book its title: "The Glories of the New Eve", being as much a tribute of gratitude to this unique Mother as it is to Her unique Daughter, 'the Bride of the Lamb of God'.

Epilogue

We just heard a Holy Father express for us once again that age-old truth: that the Resurrection and Ascension of Our Blessed Lord were the final glory due to Him for His complete victory over Sin and Death. Over "the world, the devil and the flesh".

The Dogma of the Assumption of Our Lady into Heaven has declared with infallible certainty that this, Her glory is DUE to the Mother of God because of Her role in the "common struggle" against the forces of darkness, that is, Her role as the New Eve alongside the New Adam, to secure that complete victory.

We are well advised then to expect that our own glory and our final entry into Heaven are NOT inevitable, as the Modernists teach; that no one's salvation will be secured along a different, more flabby route, but will also depend on how well each one has struggled in his or her circumstances against those very same forces of darkness: against Sin and its associates, "the world, the devil and the flesh".

"Only to a fool" will a previous Champion be "unbearable" as a sure and valuable help to achieve this personal victory and glory. Thus Catholics who "throw Her off" will be "too undisciplined," according to Sacred Scripture, to put up much of a fight of their own. Those who ARE foolish enough to exclude Her from their lives "miss Her". And it is because that She, who nowadays is so often "banished from Catholic lives into the desert of oblivion", is the "Mediatrix of all graces", that those who "miss Her injure themselves", sometimes seriously, which is the exact opposite of achieving one's final victory and glory!

In their state of debility then, such Catholics depend entirely on how well others 'stand in' for them with the New Eve of the Redemption under the cross of Jesus Christ, in cooperation with Her Victimhood.

"Many souls go to Hell because there is no one found to pray for them or to bring sacrifices for them ..."

www.ingramcontent.com/pod-product-compliance
Lightning Source LLC
Chambersburg PA
CBHW070025100426
42740CB00013B/2601